Cross-Cultural Perspectives on Reading and Reading Research

Dina Feitelson, Editor
University of Haifa
Haifa, Israel

Includes selected papers from the
Sixth IRA World Congress on Reading
Singapore
August 17-19, 1976

International Reading Association
800 Barksdale Road
Newark, Delaware   United States of America

INTERNATIONAL READING ASSOCIATION

Copyright 1978
International Reading Association, Inc.

Library of Congress Cataloging in Publication Data
World Congress on Reading, 6th, Singapore, 1976.
   Cross-cultural perspectives on reading and reading
research.
   Includes bibliographical references.
   1. Reading—Congresses. I. Feitelson, Dina.
II. International Reading Association. III. Title.
LB1049.95.W67 1976   428'.4   78-5850
ISBN 0-87207-427-7

Contents

iii

Foreword

Gradually, the International Reading Association is beginning to achieve the values of being an international association. This volume illustrates some of those values. In her introduction, Dina Feitelson makes the essential point: Most studies of learning to read and of the reading process have been carried out within the context of a limited cultural range, a single language, and a single writing system. Within such a context, it is difficult to appraise the generality, or even the meaning, of the findings. Do findings regarding the influence of letter shapes depend on the structure of the language? Does automaticity develop similarly with different writing systems? Does reading comprehension mean the same thing or require the same abilities in different languages and in different cultures? Do motivational devices that work in one culture work in another? Is an effective and logical sequence of teaching steps effective or logical in another culture or another language? If not, why not? Is there a larger, more general logic we have been missing? What is the significance, in different cultures, of being able to read? Of not being able to read?

The study of this type of question requires both an international orientation and international cooperation. The study of such questions is a proper concern of an international reading association.

This volume addresses questions that incorporate more than one culture, language, or writing system. The articles illustrate the value of this broader conceptualization of the study of reading, but they also illustrate the need for such work, for many of them represent only the important first step in the direction they explore.

If this volume illustrates the contribution the International Reading Association can make through its expanding international consciousness and program, it also illustrates the importance of a specific aspect of that program, the World Congresses. These articles are a sampling from the total program of the Sixth World Congress on Reading. Several of the articles owe their beginnings to ideas and collaboration engendered by earlier World Congresses.

The specifically international efforts of the International Reading Association are now a very small portion of the Association's program, but it is the portion with the greatest potential for expanding and reinterpreting what we "know" and for improving what we do—as students of reading, as teachers of reading, and as an association.

Walter H. MacGinitie, *President*
International Reading Association
1976-1977

Introduction

Dina Feitelson

It was only with the advent of writing—a relatively recent achievement in the history of mankind—that the vast accumulation of knowledge, which is the foundation of all modern civilization, became possible.

In the less than 6,000 years which have passed since then, written languages have become indispensable tools in many fields of human endeavour. Encoding thought, by way of graphic symbols, has made it possible to not only share ideas beyond the confines of place and time (enabling one to benefit from wisdom accumulated in remote times or far away places) but, also, to develop abstract schemes of symbolic representation, which serve as the basis for developing new fields of science—fields which were beyond the scope of imagination only a few generations ago.

It is precisely the tremendous importance of written languages in modern societies which makes all the more crucial the question of those who, as yet, can make little or no use of these modes of communication. There have been tremendous and unceasing advances in the uses to which written languages have been put; yet, these advances have not been shared by all. Swift and far reaching developments have bypassed great numbers of people in many parts of the world. Today, many countries share the problem of populations who lack necessary skills for dealing swiftly and efficiently with symbolic systems which have become integral parts of technologically advanced societies.

This lack of match between prodigious achievement on the one hand and widespread failure on the other may be at least partly due to a parallel lack of balance between efforts devoted to generating new knowledge, and efforts aimed at training people in the use of these new achievements. Nor is this a matter of material resources alone; it may well be that method, too, is at fault.

Platt's fascinating description (2) of some of the elements which make for scientific excellence includes a vision of multidisciplinary scientific establishments, protected from outside pressures and bureaucratic interference, linked to one another by fast communication channels. According to Platt, scientists in the fastest developing fields interact principally "by telephone or by face to face contact on their frequent trips" because the publication and indexing lag has made obsolete other modes of communication. By comparison, research concerned with spreading knowledge (or teaching) seems still to be in its early infancy.

In their impressive survey of educational research in seven European countries, Malmquist and Grundin (1) have well documented this fact even in regard to countries which, in relation to others, must be considered to have well developed educational systems and ample resources.

In the present context we will deal with only one aspect of this unsatisfactory state of affairs. So far, the bulk of research on reading has been carried out within the confines of prevailing local conditions. Thus, it may well be that investigators have often remained oblivious of the factors which most affected the acquisition of reading in their respective situations. Being part of the familiar scene, these factors were taken for granted instead of becoming the focus of attention in their rightful role as crucial variables.

Only when reading research becomes more truly cross-cultural will there be hope that all variables operant in any concrete reading situation will be recognized and become the subject of thorough investigation. The aim of this volume is to make a contribution, be it ever so small, to the ultimate attainment of this goal. It is also hoped that the reader will gain a somewhat better understanding of the great potential of well conducted, rigorous, cross-cultural research as well as an appreciation of the problems besetting such research.

Except for one, the papers in this volume were presented at the International Reading Association's Sixth World Congress on

Reading held in Singapore in August 1976. One additional study, by Ned Ratekin, was presented at the Twenty-First Annual Convention of the International Reading Association held in Anaheim in May 1976.

The editor wishes to thank Lloyd Kline, Faye Branca, and Romayne McElhaney for their advice and help throughout the development of this volume, especially for their good offices in rendering in readable English the papers of those of us for whom English is not a native language.

References

1. Malmquist, E., and H. U. Grundin. *Educational Research in Europe Today and Tomorrow.* Amsterdam: CWK Gleerup, 1975.
2. Platt, J. R. "Science As a Chain-Reaction," in J. R. Platt (Ed.), *The Step to Man.* New York: Wiley, 1966.

PART ONE

Examples of Cross-Cultural Research on Reading

The Bulcock, Clifton, and Beebe study opens Part One, and it is an excellent example of the kind of broadly conceived, sophisticated, rigorous scholarship which, hopefully, will become more prevalent. The results fully justify the great effort invested in this study and they prove the importance of retesting previously accepted educational truths under different circumstances. The findings that reading clearly emerges as the all important factor in school attainment, and that it is within the power of educators to improve performance in this area, will be welcomed by researchers in reading.

Next comes an advance report of an international study on cloze procedures and reading comprehension conducted by Hans Grundin from Sweden; Takahiko Sakamoto from Japan; Brother Leonard Courtney from Canada; and Judith Langer, Robert Pehrsson, and Alan Robinson from the United States. This study well illustrates some of the problems of large scale international research efforts, when even baseline points of departure (for example, grade affiliation) do not necessarily ensure uniformity in age or in years of school attendance across school systems in different countries.

A further example of this difficulty appears in the chapter by Malmquist in Part Two. Because children in Sweden start first grade at age seven, the terms *preschool* and *nursery school* in Malmquist's report denote educational frameworks for six-year-olds. Moreover, Malmquist found that lowering by one year the age of starting formal instruction in reading did not result in harmful side effects. He says, in effect, that age six—the age at which formal instruction in reading begins in most countries—is indeed suitable. Liu mentions that, according to Chinese custom, age is not counted the way it is in Western cultures, so that so called six-year-olds may well be a bit younger. One realizes, then, in well conducted cross-cultural work every possible variable will have to be checked out and controlled if a study is to yield hoped for information. Otherwise, it may mislead the unsuspecting investigator. Small wonder then that Grundin and his teammates found that much additional work will be required before well tested assessment techniques, such as the cloze procedure, can be transferred from language to language with impunity.

The studies by Ratekin and by Dzen Gross further confirm the trend established in the study by Bulcock and his coworkers. Each shows that, in its respective field of inquiry, long held beliefs were overturned by a shift to new environmental conditions. Further, in all three studies, the new findings lead to a reversal of well established findings and to an essentially more optimistic outlook, in that ascriptive variables like sex and SES do not seem to predetermine reading achievement to the extent accepted as inevitable on the basis of studies conducted in the United States.

Nilagupta's study compares the influence of syntax on readability for Thai students studying English as a second language to results obtained for native speakers of English. This study is an additional example of the way even a relatively simple transfer of research locale broadens perspectives and refines insights. The study also is a welcome reminder that, in certain educational systems, large numbers of subjects are often easily attainable and educational research can be pursued at not too high a cost.

The studies by Root and Greenlaw, concluding Part One, are concerned with issues discussed again in Part Three. By applying quantitative empirical methods to problems often discussed only in qualitative terms, these studies should result in action. An extension of the studies in other countries would certainly be of interest. Judging from Cohen's work in progress in Israel, it would seem that the tendency to portray in superficial stereotypes persons not of one's own culture, is unfortunately prevalent in children's literature in many countries. On the other hand, the problem of a lack of translated children's books may be peculiar to very large countries only. In small countries, with limited potential readership, the cost of publishing translated books is much lower than that of issuing original works. In such countries, therefore, the shoe may well be on the other foot—namely, there is a relative abundance of translated books but too few which depict local conditions familiar to young readers.

Reading Competency as a Predictor of Scholastic Performance: Comparisons between Industrialized and Third World Nations

*Jeffrey W. Bulcock**
Rodney A. Clifton
Mona J. Beebe
Memorial University
St. John's, Newfoundland, Canada

This paper is organized as follows: Part One presents the research rationale. The problem from sociological, reading research, and cross-cultural perspectives is identified; the research objectives are formulated; and the three arguments composing the explanatory framework of the structure of scholastic performance are introduced (the socializing differences, language factors, and Piagetian thinking stage arguments). Part Two is composed of three subsections: one formulating an auxiliary model, one describing the mode of analysis, and one presenting the research results. Part Three discusses the theoretical implications of the results and suggests some policy implications.

---
*We are grateful to the Council of the International Association for the Evaluation of Educational Achievement (IEA), under whose auspices the data used in this study were collected.

I. RESEARCH RATIONALE

The Problem

The problem is identified from three perspectives: sociological, reading research, and cross-cultural. The paper focuses on the problem of trying to identify a set of common elements which explain the variability in the multiple subject matter outcomes of schooling. Four sociological emphases in addressing this problem and three associated consequences are briefly referred to.

In the first place, the sociologists' primary concern in addressing the problem of cognitive outcomes of schooling has been to promote particular schools of sociological/social psychological thought. Each school has identified one or more operationalized determinants of scholastic achievement congruent with its theoretical emphasis, which intervene between the home backgrounds of pupils and their eventual subject matter competencies.

Second, increased emphasis on the inequality theme in education has resulted in close examination of the stratifying effects of differential group memberships (socioeconomic status, sex, ethnicity/race, and innercity/suburban/nonurban residence) on a range of intellectual competencies. The notion is that equal educational opportunity exists if, and only if, the criteria used in determining educational access and performance are made without reference to group memberships; that is, where group membership-school achievement relationships are effectively zero.

Third, it is noted that sociological research into these matters has represented discipline oriented, in contrast with policy oriented, research. Problems originate in the discipline or, more accurately, the "school of thought" within the discipline. Research results are used to extend disciplinary frontiers, to enhance personal academic reputations, and to maintain institutional prestige. The rules of the academic games governing competition for the scarce resources—colleague esteem, international recognition, and research grants—were played in the familiar academic arena.

Fourth, the large scale research efforts in this direction, and the host of carbon copy small scale studies which followed them, are well known and so are some of the disappointing social policy interventions which flowed from them. One consideration accounting for the discouraging results of educational policies designed to reduce educational inequalities through the promotion of compensatory educational treatments, is that few of the sociologically important intervening variables have short term policy relevance. Thus, though biosocial, symbolic interactionist or reference group theories of school achievement have generated operationalized intervening variables [such as 1) ability and motivation, 2) self-concept and teacher prophecies, 3) significant other's influence and ambition respectively], they have proved little more manageable by policymakers and educational practitioners than "fixed" or noncontrollable social background factors.

The doctrinal reactions to educational reforms by the ultra-conservatives (the Black Papers in England are one example) and the new Marxists (such as Bowles and Gintis in the United States), have created an unanticipated pincer-like movement which remains unchallenged by the public schools. Consequences resulting from efforts to document school effectiveness were the largely negative findings of the Coleman et al. report (1966) and the Jencks et al. study (1972).

While crisis symptoms abound, modest but positive responses representing a middle way persist. One such procedure involves the monitoring of innovative social policy legislation designed to solve problems. Evaluation of innovation provides an information base which may lead to further innovation requiring further evaluation and so on—a procedure leading to progressively more rational solutions. The International Association for the Evaluation of Educational Achievement (IEA) has a mandate, through its charter, for such action.[1] In a series of recent technical reports, the predictive value of language factors in causal models of scholastic performance has been noted. In particular, the impact of reading competency on multiple subject matter achievements has been impressive.

Reading operates as an intervening variable in the structure of scholastic performance in much the same way as some of the sociological variables, except that it may be several times more powerful. Thus, the influence of social background factors may be almost entirely mediated by reading comprehension. One purpose of this study is to familiarize the reading research community with recent IEA related research in the reading area.

From a reading research perspective we note that, before the beginning of the present decade, descriptions of the processes underlying the successful acquisition of reading competencies were dominated by "basic skills" explanations which were, for the most part, policy-oriented. Thus, the research problems examined originated in the world of the educational practitioner and the research results were destined for return to the real world of educational practice. Russell (45) was representative of this approach, which supported the notion that reading is best viewed as a *precise* process involving the detailed and sequential perception and identification of letters, words, spelling patterns, and large language units. The notion was congruent with the belief that underlying comprehension in early reading are a number of basic skills such as meaning vocabulary, word recognition, and grammatical usage which constitute the key ingredients in the effective teaching of reading.

We note, too, that psycholinguistic theories of reading behaviour have been formulated in the interim which, it is claimed, constitute alternative explanations of the reading process (1). We have been particularly impressed by the seminal work of the Goodman's (22,23, 24,26) and Goodman and Burke (25,27) who stand with Carroll (11,12) and Smith (47,48,49) at the juncture of two disciplinary-oriented traditions: 1) that stemming from the work of cognitive psychologists, such as Hochberg (31,32) and Kolers (34), and 2) that stemming from the work of structural linguists, such as Bloomfield (5), Fries (21), and Lefevre (35), and the transformational linguists, such as Wardhaugh (57). In contrast with "basic skills" explanations, psycholinguists conceptualize reading as a *selective* procedure; as one in which the reader uses only part of what is on the printed page, plus what he already knows about the structure of language, and whatever background knowledge and experience he can marshal in order to gain meaning from graphic display.

Thus, the Goodmans' posit that reading involves more than merely the identification of letters and words plus their associated meanings in a precise and sequential manner. Rather, they note and demonstrate that reading involves the utilization of these cueing strategies in the selective processing of available information; namely, information involving a) the configuration of letters in a line of print, sentence, or paragraph; b) the syntactic or grammatical cues inherent in that line, sentence, or paragraph; c) the semantic or meaning cues associated with the reading material; and d) the interrelationships of a), b), and c) with the reader's background of conceptual and language data.[2]

Just as we suspect that language factor and social-psychological explanation of subject matter competencies may be complementary explanations, so we suspect that basic skills and psycholinguistic explanations of reading behaviour may be complementary rather than competing approaches. A second purpose of this study, then, is to consider the contributions of reading research to explanations of individual variability in reading comprehension, and the extent to which reading comprehension mediates the effects of social background factors on a range of logically distinct subject matter outcomes of schooling.

From a cross-cultural perspective, the question arises as to the replicability in culturally diverse systems of the basic model of the structure of scholastic performance, formulated in one national system. In particular, the question arises as to the extent to which reading competency as an intervening variable operates in a consistent fashion across cultural boundaries to account for schooling achievements.

We regard such questions as extensions of the pioneering work of Gray (28), who examined the behaviour and processes in reading and writing in different cultures and, more recently, as complementary to the comparative reading studies by Thorndike (51) and Downing (16). Like these prior studies, we anticipate that the present research will raise more questions than it resolves.

Research Objectives

There has been no large scale attempt to assess the relative effect of reading as an intervening variable in models of the structure of scholastic performance in diverse cultural settings. In this study the subject matter outcomes of interest are the natural sciences—physics, chemistry, biology—and practical work. International variables—that is, variables with the same metric, gathered by standardized instruments in different countries—are used to provide a tentative answer to the

Bulcock and others

question, "Is the structure of scholastic achievement in the natural sciences the same in India (a Third World country) as in England (an industrialized country) for fourteen-year-old boys?" At this stage of our work, the emphasis is a disciplinary one. Though we anticipate that the research findings will eventually have significant policy making implications for action programmes directed at within-system, and within-school resource allocation practices, we do not address ourselves to the policy implications of the findings in detail.

In broad terms, the objective of the study is to find preliminary answers to several sets of perplexing questions concerned with the relative effects of differential socialization, language factors, and thinking stage explanations of performances in the natural sciences. Special emphasis is given to the relative effectiveness of reading competency as a predictor of scholastic performance. These questions include the following:

1. To what extent is reading comprehension an independent function of the social background characteristics of pupils?

2. To what extent is reading comprehension an independent function of a) the acquisition of such basic language skills as meaning vocabulary and b) the pupil's Piagetian thinking stage?

3. To what extent do meaning vocabulary and thinking stage factors attenuate the relative effects of socioeconomic and other social background characteristics of pupils on reading comprehension?

4. To what extent does reading comprehension, as a reasoning resource, mediate the effects of background factors, meaning vocabulary, and thinking stage; a) for achievement in science, b) for achievement in chemistry, c) for achievement in biology, d) for achievement in practical work in science, and e) for achievement in general science—a composite of a) through d)? In other words, to what extent is the covariance between every possible two-way combination of the four natural science outcomes of schooling, a function of the direct and indirect effects of the backgrond characteristics, meaning vocabulary levels, thinking stage, and reading as a set of common causes?

5. What are the similarities and differences between fourteen-year-old boys in England and India regarding the aforementioned objectives? The answers to these questions will provide additional insights into the class biased schools thesis, the language factor and learning thesis, and the thinking stage and science achievement thesis.

Explanations

In this section of the paper, three commonly asserted arguments promotive of scholastic excellence are examined. Though the proponents of these arguments tend to assume that each represents a discrete perspective, they will be treated eclectically for heuristic purposes. The explanations are referred to as: the socializing differences argument, the language factors argument, and the thinking stage argument. Underlying these arguments is the common theme that the family and the school successively and jointly provide the treatments whereby the biological, social psychological, and economic resources of children are converted into school related competencies which, in turn, constitute the resources convertible through appropriate opportunity structures into subsequent socioeconomic career attainments. For example, if reading in the Thorndikes' sense (50,53), as reasoning, is distributed unequally, its translation into subject matter performances will be distributed unequally.

1. *Socializing differences.* The socialization argument is based on the simple premise that there are considerable within- and between-group differences in child rearing; especially in terms of the learning environments and the associated economic and psychological support conditions provided within the family. Such differences govern the impact of schooling on the cognitive, affective, and conative outcomes of schooling. The notion is that the child's resources are converted into additional resources (assets or liabilities) through interaction with the within-classroom learning environments. Eventually, the effectiveness of the within-family and within-school socializing treatments determines the variability in the zero sum distribution of scarce societal resources such as school achievement, social prestige, and income. One such school related and, hence, policy manageable resource, is reading competency.

The extreme socializing differences position holds that a child's progress through school is more a function of social class (the father's status in the occupational order) than of meritocratic criteria such as ability, effort, and motivation. The three factors commonly used as measures of the effects of social backgrounds are father's occupation (the socioeconomic status variable), mother's and father's (or parental) education, and the family configuration (the number *and* spacing of children).

In meaning vocabulary terms, the effect of the socioeconomic variable is attributable to the fact that socioeconomic status is a proxy for environmental complexity and cultural enrichment. Thus it is noted, in the first instance, that children from relatively complex home socializing environments have the opportunity to develop more precocious meaning vocabularies through the necessity of being initiated into the common language meanings that such environments hold for their members. It is also noted that material deprivation is highly correlated with cultural impoverishment—at least in those economic systems with highly developed commutative mechanisms—and that the child's cultural circumstances will determine the opportunity at home for learning and practicing school relevant behaviours.

In reading comprehension terms, though socioeconomic status will have modest net effects on reading, its major impact will be an indirect one as mediated by the meaning vocabulary variable.

A similar logic prevails in the case of the other background factors—parental education and family configuration. Thus, children whose parents are well-educated and, hence, highly articulate, are likely to utilize more precocious language skills and codes than children whose parents are less well educated, ceteris paribus. It is believed that the importance of early language learning for intellectual growth is more likely to be stressed and recognized by well-educated mothers and that these mothers will be more skillful in the transmission of the primary learning elements required for decoding/encoding precocity than their less well-educated counterparts.

The family configuration subargument (*60, 61*), is based on the postulate that different family configurations constitute different intellectual environments; hence, formulation of the proposition that, if the intellectual environment is the aggregate level of all family members' absolute intellectual contribution, then not only does it change continually as the children develop, but is a function of the number of additions or departures from the family and the spacing of children. The intellectual environment of the family is captured by the family configuration variable which will be related to vocabulary, thinking stage, and reading resource acquisitions of children.

2. *The language factors argument.* Family socializing differences explanations address the question of how family environments both account for and translate the unequal biological, linguistic, and socioeconomic resources of children into unequal educational attainments. Language factors such as those represented by basic skills and psycholinguistic explanations of reading competency constitute the basic learning resources of children. These language factors include the cueing strategy variables (grapho-phonic, syntactic, and semantic cues) and the basic skills variables (meaning vocabulary, word recognition, and grammatical usage), though their interrelationships in terms of reading comprehension outcomes are imperfectly understood. Nevertheless, they constitute linguistic resource assets which are inequitably distributed and which account to some considerable extent for the fact that children entering school each year do so with different levels of the resouces required as prerequisites to successful performances during the year.

In the general case, the greater the linguistic resource assets of the pupil in terms of coping with the progressively more complex environments of the school — especially in terms of subject matter complexity — and the more effective the teacher treatments in relation to these primary resources, the greater the probability that the individual will receive preferred treatment in the different settings at later grade levels. It follows that the primary linguistic resources are translatable in school settings into additional resources such as reading competencies, which in the form of "reading as reasoning" constitute a secondary resource asset. Reading on a priori grounds is a common cause of the multiple subject matter achievements of pupils at the upper elementary and secondary school levels. It is the relative magnitude of this dependency which is assessed in the present study.

The dependence of subject matter performance on reading resources has been demonstrated in several studies. Thus, Hauser (*30*: 77-80) showed that the reading comprehension of Tennessee high school students was a powerful intervening variable mediating the distal effects of family background factors and mathematics and that the direction of the relationship was recursive, not reciprocal. Similarly, verbal reasoning is shown to mediate background variables and the relative importance of parents, teachers, and peers as sources of psychological support in accounting for the observed educational inequalities of Canadian high school students (59). Thorndike (51: 169) notes that inequalities in science and literature achievements are mediated by reading comprehension, and postulates that reading plays a key role as a predictor agent for more specific subject matter areas.

The linguistic factor thesis has been powerfully demonstrated in causal models of school achievement in literature by Bulcock (7), and Bulcock and Finn (10). The importance of meaning vocabulary levels as predictors of the multiple outcomes of science performances (physics, chemistry, biology, and practical work) has been shown in a series of multivariate models by Finn and Mattsson (19). Both meaning vocabulary levels and reading competencies were shown to be powerful intervening variables in multivariate models of the structure of scholastic performance in science and literature by Bulcock (8) and Bulcock and Beebe (9). These studies, sponsored by the Institute for the Study of International Problems in Education, University of Stockholm, utilize national level probability samples of fourteen-year-olds from Sweden and England selected from the IEA data archive.

3. *The thinking stage argument.* The Piagetian thinking stage argument is invoked for two reasons. In the first place, we accept the postulate that scientific understanding is, on a priori grounds, dependent on a) development of the logic of propositions and b) acquisition of the operations of combinations and proportions, that is, the hypothetico-deductive mode of thinking (40). Thus, failure to take the thinking stage argument into account in explaining achievement in the natural sciences would constitute a serious conceptual limitation in the develoment of a model of the structure of scholastic performance.

We have argued in our description of the epigenesis of language in the resource conversion context that reading resources are required as a function of the prior transformation of linguistic resources through both cueing strategy and basic skills approaches. The argument was extended on a priori grounds, such that achievements in the natural sciences were at least a partial function of reading competency; that is, the relationship between reading competency and natural science achievement is positive. It was also postulated that the relationship was a recursive one, such that science achievement is dependent on the development of reading competency but not the other way around.

Thus, the position is held that both language factors and thinking stage arguments have to be given independent consideration on the basis of the assumption that they are complementary, not competing sources of explanation.[3] Thus, the thinking stage argument is invoked as a secondary concern, in order to establish the legitimacy of the language factors argument when both are taken into account. The relation between reading and science achievement might otherwise be spurious.

II. RESEARCH DESIGN AND FINDINGS

Model Formulation

The extent to which socializing differences, language factors, and thinking stage explanations account for the covariation between natural science achievements, and the extent to which these explanations are complementary or competing approaches, is examined through the analysis of a recursive model designed to map the complexities underlying scientific understanding. The model may be subdivided into four segments: 1) meaning vocabulary as dependent, three source variables congruent with the socializing differences argument—father's occupational status, parental education, and family size—as independent; 2) thinking stage as dependent, the three source variables and meaning vocabulary as independent; 3) reading comprehension as dependent, the three source variables, meaning vocabulary, and thinking stage as independent; and 4) physics, chemistry, biology, and practical work, each as dependent outcomes simultaneously considered as a function of a set of common predictors—the source variables, meaning vocabulary, thinking stage, and reading comprehension. The complexity of these pathways is illustrated in a basic conceptual model followed by an elaborated version of the model in Figure 1.

Figure 1. Basic and Elaborated Conceptual Models Illustrating the Relationships between Variables Suggested by Socializing Differences, Language Factors, and Thinking Stage Arguments, Explaining School Achievement in the Natural Sciences.

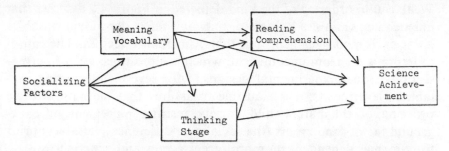

Figure 1.1. Basic Conceptual Model of School Achievement in the Natural Sciences Illustrating the Pivotal Position of Reading as an Intervening Variable.

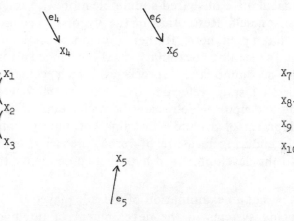

Figure 1.2. Elaborated Model of School Achievement in the Natural Sciences.[a]

---

[a]Where: X_1 = father's occupational status; X_2 = parental education; X_3 = size of family; X_4 = meaning vocabulary; X_5 = thinking stage; X_6 = reading comprehension; X_7 = physics; X_8 chemistry; X_9 = biology; X_{10} = practical work. Note the flow of effect in Figure 1.2, in which each variable is affected by all those to the left of it, and where no causal assumptions are made about the source variables or the outcome variables which are shown in vertical columns.

In anticipation of criticism, two rejoinders are advisable at this point to prevent unnecessary misinterpretation. In the first instance, it is desirable to address the structural equation commandment that there shall be no ambiguity in the causal ordering of the variables. Weak causal ordering of the kind depicted in Figure 1.2 assumes that independent variables X_j may (or may not) affect dependent variables X_i at each model segment, but that X_i cannot affect X_j. The causal ordering is far from unequivocal, which is almost necessary in cross-sectional, quasiexperimental designs, with several intervening variables. Nevertheless, it is plausible to assume that the natural cycle ordering of the parent-child variety justifies placement of background factors and events (the socializing differences variables) prior to outcomes dependent on more recent events and experiences.

What is more problematic is the relationship between language (in which words as representations of existential reality facilitate the development and redevelopment of meanings) and thought—especially verbal thought, facilitative of shared communication with others and interpretations of oneself. Resolution of the Vygotsky versus Piaget dilemma is not attempted here. Rather, a compromise solution is attempted. A child's meaning vocabulary is well-developed prior to the dual assimilative-accommodation processes which generate that epigenetic intellectual stage referred to as the formal operational stage of thinking and upon which scientific understanding depends. Thus, the development of a child's meaning vocabulary, conceived of as a relatively enduring measure of verbal precocity, is chronologically prior to the development of hypothetico-deductive thought processes.

One regret is that an examination of the role played by the psycholinguistic cueing systems in the development of intelligence is not possible given the IEA data base. We harbour the hunch that it might be considerable; in which case much current research on the language/thought controversy is misspecified due to the erroneous omission of important variables.

There is still the problem of the relationship between thinking stage and reading comprehension. In this issue we have followed our Canadian colleague Hildred Rawson (43) who examined the contributions of five logical operations—conservation, classification, deduction, induction, and probability reasoning—to the reading performances of fourth grade pupils (nine- and ten-years-old) and the implicit assumptions in Thorndike's classic study (50). While the possibility must be entertained that a functional or reciprocal relationship exists between thinking stage and reading, this hypothesis—though eminently testable—is not examined in this research. It seems that the thinking/reading relationship is not resolvable on a priori grounds and must, therefore, remain as an outstanding research issue.

The second rejoinder concerns the isomorphism between verbal or main theory explanations and the auxiliary or operational models deduced from them. The analyst's task is to formulate a best fitting auxiliary model to the conceptual model in such a way that the associated hypotheses are falsifiable. In this task, the admixture of theory and observation is sometimes formidable. Notwithstanding contrary claims (6), we share the position that complete isomorphism between conceptual models and their synthetic analogues is unattainable; therefore, subsequent analysis does not liberate the reader from the necessity of exercising independent judgment and a healthy scepticism.

Analytical Strategy

Instrumentation questions are briefly discussed in technical Appendix A; and the statistical results are presented in the Tables of technical Appendix B. It is hoped that by relegating routine procedural matters to the appendices, they will not interfere with substantive concerns. The evidence constituting the results is presented for the expert, but not in a way which intrudes on, or inhibits, consideration of more central concerns.

For the most part, analyses revolve around the development and test of structural equation models (3,18) designed to be isomorphic with the auxiliary models and the verbal theories explaining the aspects of reading and science performance under examination. Recursive models are tested through the estimation of model parameters using path analysis (58,17), which is a generalization of multiple linear regression estimation procedures to systems of causally related variables. The parameters are estimated as partial regression coefficients and interpreted as measures of effect.

The unstandardized regression coefficients of all intervening variables (meaning vocabulary, thinking stage, and reading comprehension) are allowed to assume a substantive meaning that is uncommon in studies composed of sets of variables, each characterized by a different metric. This is because they are to be used as percentages in a model where the four dependent variables are also percentage measures. Thus, a unit change in, say, reading comprehension, will refer to a percentage unit. Since unstandardized coefficients are interpretable as the unique influence of a variable, given controls over other variables in the model, the findings may be interpretable in such terms as: an x percent improvement in reading comprehension will produce an x percent improvement in physics, ceteris paribus, and so on. Since the effects are additive, the estimation of the effects of several predictors simultaneously makes it possible to estimate resource costs in terms of expected natural science outcomes.

Following Finney (20), a second type of analysis is conducted, in which the gross or total effects of the relationship between two variables is decomposed into three independent elements: a) the net or direct effect, b) the indirect effect, and c) a noncausal spurious component. The first two elements (a and b) may be summed to represent the total causal effects (TCEs). The utility of the TCEs lies in the fact that they represent exact estimates of the total relative impact of explanatory variables on the outcomes of interest. TCEs may be ranked for comparative purposes.

Findings

1. *England.* Zero-order relations are presented in Appendix B, Table B-1. It is noted that the association between reading and all science subtests is greater than 0.5; and that the reading overall science performance relationship has a correlation coefficient greater than 0.7. The relationships between background factors and natural science performances are as hypothesized. Thus, the coefficients in the 0.3 range for the father's occupation—natural science and father's occupation—reading relationships are about the same order of magnitude as those reported in other industrialized nations (44).

The thinking stage variable is strongly associated with achievements in the natural sciences with most coefficients in the 0.4 range.

It is useful to note that the Piagetian variable is not overly determin-
istic—a fact probably demonstrating that natural science performances in school settings do not always depend on the application of
higher order thinking processes; or, obversely, that rote recall and
knowledge of mere information will go a long way in some school
systems to account for cognitive achievements. The high correlation
(in the 0.5 range) between meaning vocabulary and subtest performances in science is particularly noteworthy in view of the emphasis
placed on language factors explanations.

The advantage of Table B-2 is that the structural coefficients
may be interpreted as measures of the unique influence of a variable,
given controls over the other variables in the model. For example,
because all the endogenous variables in the model (the intervening
variables and the outcome variables) are percentage scores, the regression coefficients may be interpreted as follows: an x percent
improvement in, say, reading will likely produce an x percent improvement in some outcome (say, overall science performance) ceteris
paribus. Take the science outcome in Table B-2. Column 1 in science
provides the regression coefficients for each of the predictor variables
in the model of scholastic performance. With the important exception
of the three source variables (FATHOCC, PARED, and SIBSZ), the
remaining predictors lend themselves to the following interpretation: a 10 percent improvement in reading comprehension will produce a 4.48 percent improvement in science performance, ceteris
paribus. Since the model is an additive one it is possible to interpret
the effects of reading and thinking in the following manner: if as a
function of teacher treatments and pupil effort a 10 percent gain in
both reading and thinking performances was accomplished, the net
expected gain in science performance would be 4.21 + 1.82 = 6.03
percent.

School systems knowing this kind of information could eventually estimate how resource costs might be weighed against expected
outcomes in their planning of school curricula. If it were thought that
language factors were more policy manageable than thinking stage
elements (e.g., more responsive to teacher treatments and the con-
comitant pupil effort), the expected impact of the combined language
factors might be contrasted with the combined impact of reading and

thinking. In this hypothetical example the language factors account for effects of .136 + .421 = .557 (versus .182 + .421 = .603) on science performance. The difference (.046) is modest. The decision to emphasize the teaching of the language arts including reading might be a sound one if thinking stage elements prove less amenable to teacher treatments than language factors. There can be little doubt, however, that the teaching of reading is of crucial importance in terms of pupil achievements in the natural sciences.

The relative effect of a predictor variable (i.e., relative to all other model predictors) is noted in Column II which reports the path coefficients. It is noted that, in terms of overall science achievement, reading has the most powerful net effect (.487), relative to the other predictors; followed by thinking (.225) and meaning vocabulary (.178) in that order. Reading has more than twice the impact on science than the thinking variable; and, incidentally, eight times the impact of father's occupation or any other background variable.

Since some of the effects of the more distal factors are mediated by intervening variables, their total casual influences may be underestimated on the basis of an examination of their structural coefficients. Following Finney (20), the total causal effect (TCE) of each predictor in the model is calculated (Table B-3) and ranked for comparative purposes (Table B-4). The utility of the TCEs lies in the fact that they represent exact estimates of the total relative impact, both direct and indirect, on the outcomes of interest.

From Column 4, Table B-3, one notes that the direct effect of father's occupational status on science is a modest .058; whereas, the total causal effect—the direct effect, plus the effect of father's occupational status on science as mediated by the intervening variables VOCAB, THINK and READ—is .259. Though the TCE of FATHOCC on SCIENCE is considerable, it is shown in Table B-4 that the TCEs of VOCAB, THINK, and READ are even greater. Similarly, it is shown in Table B-4 that the impact of the variables stemming from language factor and thinking stage explanations for the English data is considerably greater than for those stemming from socializing differences explanations.

2. *India.* It is noted from the correlation matrix (Table B-1) that reading-natural science relationships in India lack uniformity. The correlation between reading and biology is .27; correlations between

reading and physics, and reading and practical work are in the 0.3-0.4 range; and those between reading and chemistry and reading and total science performance, in the 0.4-0.5 range. Though the significance levels were less than .001, the unanticipated range in the magnitudes of the scores remains difficult to explain.

Correlations between background variables and natural science performances were well below those anticipated. While findings regarding the effects of the thinking stage variable were less problematic, the modest strength of the associations (from .10 to .25) should be noted. The range of zero-order relations between meaning vocabulary on the one hand, and the natural science achievements on the other, was consistent with the language factors explanation. Table B-2 evidence is supportive of the complementary thesis, where it is noted that the effects of the thinking stage variable on all natural science outcomes except practical work are statistically and substantively significant over-and-above the effects of the language factors explanations.

Examination of the TCEs of the source variables in India (Table B-3) confirm the negligible effects of background factors noted from their zero-order measures of association. In fact, the family configuration variable had negligible effects on all endogenous variables. The TCEs of intervening variables, with the exception of thinking as a predictor of reading and practical work, were either moderate or strong. Most were in the 0.2 to 0.4 range and sufficient to be regarded as being of substantive, as well as statistical, significance. All these relationships were in the hypothesized direction.

Note that in TCE terms the effects of the meaning vocabulary variable outranked all other effects on the natural sciences. TCEs of the reading variable were in second rank (Table B-4) and thinking stage influences were in third place. The impact of the intervening variables on practical work in science were, however, noticeably less powerful than on physics, chemistry, and biology.

3. *England/India comparisons.* Similarities clearly outweigh the differences. The most important differences to be noted concern the socializing explanation. Whereas the TCEs of father's occupational status in England on all endogenous variables were significant— six out of the eight relationships in TCE terms were greater than 0.2—the same was far from the case in India. Two of the TCEs of

father's occupational status in India were negligible; only one was above 0.1; and the remainder were between .05 and .1, which is regarded as being of marginal substantive significance.

The effects of parental education in the India sample were similarly modest. Impact on meaning vocabulary, thinking, and practical work was negligible. Though in chemistry a TCE of .113 was recorded, the remaining relationships were of marginal importance. Since all the number of children TCEs were negligible (Table B-4), the variable effectively played no part in accounting for the natural science outcomes. Such a specification error—that of erroneous inclusion—may be rectified by respecifying the model as in Figure B-1. In the respecified India model, the vocabulary and thinking variables are shown as source variables since there are no associative relationships between them or between them and the remaining background factors. This leaves reading as the only mediating variable between four source variables and four natural science outcomes. The evidence supports this model respecification as being the most accurate representation of the structure of scholastic performance for fourteen-year-old boys in Hindi speaking India.[4]

A second difference between the countries concerns the extent to which antecedent variables account for variance in natural science outcomes. Though in both countries the model is obviously an effective one for accounting for science achievement, the explanatory power of the English application ($100R^2 = 59.5$) is greater than that of the Indian ($100R^2 = 35.9$).

Similar differences are noted in terms of the extent to which the antecedent variables constitute a set of common causes accounting for the covariation between subtest performances in the natural sciences. Thus, it is noted from Table B-6 that, with the exception of the chemistry-biology relationship, the predictors in the English model of scholastic performance accounted for greater proportions of the covariance between natural science outcomes than did the common predictors in the India model. The median proportion explained in England was .45 and in India .38.

The three noted differences should not be exaggerated. Except for these, the model of scholastic achievement in the natural sciences operated in the predictable way in both countries. Reading in England was consistently the most powerful predictor of science achievements, and the same was true in India with the exception of performance in biology. Most of the time, the thinking stage variable had the next most powerful net effect when simultaneously considering the effects of all other system variables. Thinking was only marginally ahead of meaning vocabularly influences in terms of direct effects. When the indirect effects of meaning vocabulary on natural science performances as mediated by thinking and reading are considered, as in Table B-4, it is shown that its TCEs in both England and India rank in first place.

III. INTERPRETATIONS

Theoretical Implications

In England, but not in India, reading was significantly influenced by variables generated by socializing differences arguments. Even in England the direct effects of the three family background variables on reading were of modest magnitude. Their total causal effects, however, were several times larger as shown in Table B-3. Since the TCE of father's occupational status on reading for the English sample was considerable, the question arises whether English schools are class biased institutions; that is, whether socioeconomic status is more important than merit in determining school achievement.

The importance of the question stems from the fact that if English schools are class biased, the societal effort necessary to implement educational reforms will be of a different order of magnitude than if the schools themselves control the reformist mechanisms. Background variables are not in the short term amenable to policy intervention. To clarify the problem, three sources of evidence are available. First, zero-order relationships are presented between the first five predictor variables in the model and reading.

Data in Table 1 from the IEA/U.S. sample are included for comparative purposes. Second, the direct effects of the predictors are shown in a path model (Figure 2). Third, the total causal effect coefficients of the preditors presented in Table B-4 are compared.

The zero-order relationships between father's occupation and reading, and meaning vocabulary and reading, are the same in the

Table 1
Zero-Order Relationships between Five Predictor Variables
and Reading: England/India/U.S. Comparisons [a]

Relationship	England	India	U.S.
r_{16}	.295	.013	.306
r_{26}	.129	.031	.310
r_{36}	-.166	.033	-.096
r_{46}	.647	.364	.666
r_{56}	.365	.087	(b)

[a] Where X_1 = FATHOCC, X_2 = PARED, X_3 = SIBSZ, X_4 = VOCAB, X_5 = THINK, and X_6 = READ.

[b] The r_{56} relationship is not available for the United States. The THINK variable was constructed from the distractors to four science test items, but in the United States fourteen-year-olds who wrote the IEA science test did not write the IEA reading comprehension test. This means that the structure of scholastic performance model cannot be tested using the IEA/U.S. data.

industrialized nations of England and the United States. Relationships between parental education and reading, and between number of children and reading are different in the industrialized nations. Though different background variables have different effects, they are all outranked in magnitude by the effect on reading of the meaning vocabulary variable.

A more stringent test of the class bias thesis involves examination of the relative effect of each predictor while simultaneously taking other predictors into account. Such a test is presented in Figure 2 where it is shown that father's occupational status is a more powerful predictor of reading than the other background factors, and that the effects of meaning vocabulary and thinking stage variables on reading are over six times and two times as powerful, respectively, as the father's occupation variable.

It must be recognized, however, that some of the effects of the background factors on reading are indirect. For example, father's

Figure 2. Path Model of Reading Comprehension in England and India.[a]

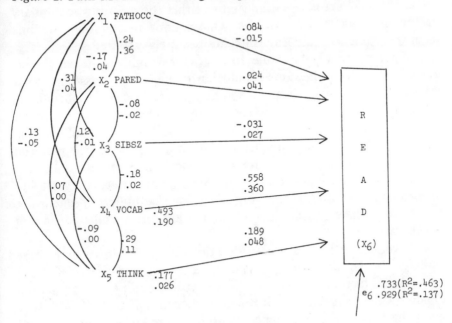

[a] Path coefficients are presented above the paths. The top coefficient is for England in each case. The regression coefficients for VOCAB and THINK only, are presented below the paths (cf. Table B-2).

occupation influences meaning vocabulary; similarly, it influences thinking stage development; and it influences reading via these mediating pathways. In view of the potentially powerful indirect effects of the background variables, it becomes important to examine their total causal effects as presented in Table B-4. It is noted that the direct effects are underestimates of the total effect of the background factors.

Nevertheless, Table B-4 evidence does not support a class biased interpretation, but rather a language factor bias. The TCE ranking of FATHOCC is behind that of VOCAB, but more important is the fact that the TCE for FATHOCC is less than half that of VOCAB. It is inferred from these (Table B-4) results that the three explanations are complementary, not competing, notions. They are necessary, but not sufficient, for explaining variability in reading in England.

Though socializing differences variables are of substantive importance, their impact is less than that of either the meaning vocabulary or the thinking stage variables. One cannot reasonably conclude from this evidence that English schools are class biased.

Application of the same logic to the English natural science outcomes results in the same conclusion insofar as the class bias thesis is concerned. What seems problematic is the failure of the socializing differences explanation in the case of India. The effects of the social background variables meaning vocabulary, thinking, and reading are negligible. Literally, this means that in India neither the material circumstances of the home, nor differences in parental education, nor the family configuration in terms of size, have effects on variation in meaning vocabulary, thinking stage, or reading comprehension. On the other hand, thinking and reading are influenced by meaning vocabulary.

Several ex post facto considerations are compatible with these findings. In the first place, it is conceivable that the effects of social background factors may already have occurred prior to Indian school children's reaching the age of fourteen. Second, Thorndike (52) suggests that reading performances in India were sufficiently low that the children were unable to read the student questionnaires and that, therefore, many students resorted to random guessing. On the other hand, the language and thinking stage arguments were supported. For purposes of analysis those students reading below a designated level of performance were eliminated from the sample as is pointed out in Appendix B. For these reasons the random guessing explanation might be discounted.

Third, it is important to note that describing selected characteristics of a family is not the same as describing the socializing mechanisms, that is, how a family socializes children. It is conceivable that family characteristics in India fail to operate as viable proxies for family socializing treatments as in industrialized nations. Alternatively, there may be no significant differences in the socializing treatments preferred in Hindi-speaking India on the basis of socioeconomic differences; in which case the support for a null hypothesis is real, not spurious. Before reaching such a conclusion, however, further research is desirable. It is prudent not to prejudge in these important matters, especially because socializing differences explanations of natural science performances in India are viable. Note from Table B-4 the TCEs of father's occupational status on physics, and overall science performances; and the TCE of parental education on chemistry.

The fourth objective of this research is important because it concerns the relative effect of reading performance on natural science performances while taking other determinants of science achievement into account simultaneously. Another way of stating the objective is as follows: To what extent are socializing differences, language factors, and thinking stage explanations of achievements in the natural sciences complementary or competing arguments? As was pointed out in the findings section, the three arguments in the case of both countries are complementary—each has to be considered. In view of the magnitude of the independent effects of reading on science outcomes, however, the relationship deserves special consideration.

The view is held that the findings represent prima facie support for the Thorndikes' postulate (50,53), namely, that "performance in reading, at least after the basic decoding skills are mastered, is primarily an indicator of the general level of the individual's thinking and reasoning processes rather than a set of distinct and specialized skills." It is reading in this sense that accounts for its effectiveness as a common determinant of the covariation between the natural science subtest performances (Table B-5).

Though the Thorndikes describe the relationship between reading and reasoning, thereby justifying their synonymy, it is the Goodmans who account for the process underlying reading as reasoning. Their cueing strategy thesis is congruent with the reasoning thesis in that it describes the selective processes used in the reading act which are paradigmatic of the reasoning process. Application of cueing strategies involve reactions to printed material in a number of ways— checking validity, making inferences, drawing conclusions—all of which may be regarded as reasoning. Thus, although the Goodman thesis is not tested in this research, it promoted the formulation of the research hypotheses, and the findings are congruent with the "guessing game" reading thesis.

Undoubtedly, however, the effects of reading on natural science achievements were attenuated by the thinking stage factor. In both

Table 2
Percentage Effects of Language Factors and Thinking Stage
Variables on Natural Science Performances[a]

Effect of a 10 per cent increase in:		Outcomes (%)				
		Physics	Chemistry	Biology	Practical	Science
X_4 VOCAB	E	1.2	1.6	1.1	1.5	1.4
	I	1.7	1.1	1.3	1.2	1.3
X_5 THINK	E	1.7	2.0	2.2	1.4	1.8
	I	1.1	1.4	1.2	0.2	1.0
X_6 READ	E	4.8	4.0	3.4	4.5	4.2
	I	4.2	4.6	2.0	3.2	3.5
Combined language factors (X_4+X_6)	E	6.0	5.6	4.52	6.0	5.6
	I	5.9	5.7	3.3	4.4	4.8
Combined language factors & thinking stage $(X_4+X_5+X_6)$	E	7.8	7.6	6.7	7.4	7.4
	I	7.0	7.1	4.5	4.6	5.8

[a]The table may be read as follows: a 10 percent increase in reading will account for a 4.2 percent increase in science performance for English fourteen-year-old boys or a 3.5 percent increase in science performance for Indian fourteen-year-old boys, ceteris paribus. Similarly, if the three factors VOCAB, THINK, and READ each could be simultaneously improved by 10 percent, the resultant effect on science performance would probably be in the region of 7.4 percent in England and 5.8 percent in India, ceteris paribus.

countries, the thinking variable proved a powerful determinant of science over and above all other predictors. The percentage effect estimates of the three intervening variables are presented in Table 2. It will be noted that in physics and chemistry their combined effects are about the same in both England and India. In biology, practical work, and science, the combined effects of language factor and thinking stage variables are more powerful in England than in India. Since the intervening variables—especially the reading variable—are the ones most manageable by school authorities, and since these variables have decidedly greater influence than the background factors in TCE terms, there seems little doubt that schools may be held accountable for pupil performances in the natural sciences. Further, the importance of reading precocity as the single most powerful mediating variable in the flow of effects accounting for natural science achievements cannot be doubted on the basis of IEA evidence.

CONCLUSIONS

This paper attempted:

1. to formulate and test a general model of the structure of scholastic performance;
2. to popularize the notion of reading as a school dependent personality resource asset, readily convertible in classroom treatment settings into additional desired scholastic performances;
3. to demonstrate the pivotal role that reading, as reasoning, plays in accounting for natural science achievements in physics, chemistry, biology, practical work, and an overall science performance composite;
4. to test the proposition that socializing differences, language factors, and thinking stage arguments are complementary rather than competing explanations of school achievements in the content fields;
5. to assess the extent to which reading as a school dependent resource translates the unequal socioeconomic and linguistic resources of children into unequal natural science achievements; and
6. to examine the operation of the structure of scholastic performance model in two culturally and economically different nations—England and India.

It was concluded that the socializing differences argument was defensible in England, but it was less so in India. The extreme socializing differences argument that a child's progress through school is more a function of social class than ability and motivation was rejected. The linguistic resources of children and their stage of thinking had effects on the natural science performances of children which were greater in magnitude in both England and India than social background factors.

Several ex post facto explanations of the almost negligible impact of social background factors in India on reading competency and science achievements were considered. Two explanations seemed worthy of further investigation. The first notion holds that by the age of fourteen the effects of social circumstances in India may already have operated and that those boys with severe social handicaps may have already withdrawn from formal schooling. The second explanation concerns the differences between what home circumstances are and what they do. Thus, in India the social background factors may not operate as adequate proxies for the differences in the actual socializing treatments provided in the home. Alternatively, home socializing treatments may be more uniform in India than in England across socioeconomic status boundaries.

Because language factors and thinking stage arguments were independently operative in accounting for science performance, it was concluded that the three autonomous explanations of scholastic performances complemented one another. As expected, the Piagetian position that achievements in the sciences are dependent upon the attainment of formal operational thought was strongly supported in both countries. The test was a stringent one in that the Piagetian variable operated over and above simultaneous consideration of five other contenders. Of these other contenders, however, the language factors proved particularly powerful. Language factor arguments were traced to the recent work of R. L. Thorndike, Goodman, and Goodman. While there are few parallels this century to the sustained intellectual effort in developmental psychology of Jean Piaget, the results of this research suggest that Thorndike's work in educational psychology and Kenneth Goodman's work in applied psycholinguistics also merit careful attention.

The results of this research show that reading as a policy manageable variable amenable to within classroom treatments is the single most powerful mechanism known for determining school achievements in physics, chemistry, biology, practical work, and overall science performance. This is interpreted to mean that teachers —individually and collectively—may legitimately assume greater responsibility for the intellectual performances of students than heretofore and, by the same token, may be legitimately held accountable for the quality of service they provide their clientele. Because reading in both an industrialized and a Third World nation has been shown to be a crucially important resource mechanism in the structure of scholastic performances; because this mechanism accounts for the translation of socializing and linguistic resources into the additional desired resources of multiple subject-matter achievements; and since these achievements constitute important criteria in the allocation of scarce societal resources such as statuses, incomes, and associated psychological satisfactions, it is easily concluded that no teacher is more important than the reading teacher.

Attention might be given to the political implications of these findings. Individually, reading teachers play crucial roles in the initiation of pupils into the logic of reasoning. Collectively, reading teachers represent a powerful political force. The evidence suggests that there may be no more subtle way of impoverishing the cultural resources of a society than by placing constraints on the opportunities that children have for learning how to read. Conversely, there would seem to be no more effective way of liberating the intellect, of overcoming cultural impoverishment, than through the development of reading competency, and ipso facto of reason.

Footnotes

1. IEA, incorporated in 1967 under Belgian law, is a nonprofit, nongovernmental organization which undertakes educational and related research on an international scale in order to examine educational problems common to many countries and to provide evidence which may help the improvement of educational systems. Major studies by IEA analysts include: Husen (33); Bloom (4); Comber and Keeves (14); Thorndike (51); Purves (42); Peaker (38); Carroll (13); Torney, et al. (54); Lewis and Massad (36); Passow, et al. (37); and Walker (56).
2. Note that mathematics is similarly involved with both syntactic and semantic cueing elements along with the grapho-phonic. It may be that problem solving skills (or intuitive understanding) so valued by the mathematics teacher favouring the heuristic mode of instruction, involves the simultaneous application of mathematical syntax cues, mathematical semantic cues, and mathematical graphic cues which the Goodmans show account for the development of reading competencies.
3. The problem remembles that concerning whether language plays a determinant role in the intellectual development of children (55) or whether the development of language seems to depend on that of operations (41,46). The issue is not central to our present thesis; therefore, we wish to acknowledge the issue, but "beg the question." For opposing positions in the North American literature, one may refer to Pflaum (39) and Day (15).
4. See Peaker (38) for details for the three stage sampling design for the six Hindi speaking states sampled. These states contain approximately 41 percent of the Indian population.

TECHNICAL APPENDIX A: INSTRUMENTATION

The purpose of this appendix is twofold: 1) to describe the ten variables constituting the auxiliary model and 2) to present their frequency distributions. Where possible, the data for England and India are interposed for ease of comparison.

(1) *Variables*

X_1 FATHOCC—*Father's occupational status.* Each national center participating in the stage two, three-subject survey was asked to design its own occupational status scale on the basis of whatever national norms were considered most valid. In England, the procedure adopted was one in which professional, managerial, and business owners were ranked in categories 6 and 7; clerical workers, supervisory personnel, and service workers, in categories 5, 4, and 3; skilled blue collar in category 2, unskilled manual workers and unclassifiable personnel in categories 1 and 0.

The father's occupational code, adopted in India, was more precise in that nine categories were employed. The differences in coding, attributable to the different economic systems in the two countries, made direct comparisons impossible. In India, professional, managerial, and semiprofessionals were ranked in categories 9, 8, and 7; small businesspersons, large scale farmers, and clerical workers in categories 6, 5, and 4; semiskilled workers, farm labourers, and unskilled labourers in categories 3, 2, and 1; and those without occupations, or unclassifiable, were coded zero.

X_2 PARED—*Parental education.* Both mother's and father's education were scored on a five category scale in terms of years of schooling: 0 years, 1-5, 6-10, 11-15, and greater than 15. These variables were added in order to estimate parental education. The variable was constructed in the same manner for both countries.

X_3 SIBSZ—*Number of brothers and sisters.* In both countries, the variable was operationalized by the question: "How many brothers and sisters have you?" The response categories (1-5) were: 0, 1, 2, 3, 4 or more.

X_4 VOCAB—*Meaning vocabulary.* The IEA word knowledge test, after correction for guessing, would seem to represent an accurate within-country estimate of a pupil's meaning vocabulary, and might be considered an acceptable proxy of verbal ability (51:36). It is assumed that the variation in test scores from country to country was a function of shifts in the discrimatory power of some of the 40 test items after translation. Nevertheless, within country discrimination was satisfactory as indicated by K-R formula 20 reliability coefficients (Kuder and Richardson, 1937) of .833 for England and .812 for India. Raw scores in both countries were converted into percentages.

Table A.1

Coefficients for Scales Based on IEA Science Test Items [a]

COUNTRY	COEFFICIENTS[b]			
	1	2	3	4
England	.811	.670	.141	.427
India	.765	.675	.090	.276
U.S.A.[c]	.851	.723	.129	.464

a) Results are for those boys who could read. The readability criterion was a score greater than one of the reading comprehension test after correction for guessing; where the correction for guessing formula was R-W/K-1 (R = no. correct answers, W = no. wrong answers, K = no. alternatives in multiple choice items).

b) 1 = coefficient of reproducibility
2 = minimum marginal reproducibility
3 = percent improvement
4 = coefficient of scalability

c) U.S.A. results are provided as a second industrialized nation referent. They may provide some further reassurance that models of the kind being tested remain stable despite being tested on data from a variety of nations. It is unfortunate that, at the present stage of the ongoing research, an additional Third World referent could not be provided.

X_5 THINK—*Piagetian thinking stage.* Following Bergling (*2*), item analysis data derived from multiple-choice items on the IEA science test were used to construct a Piagetian thinking stage variable common to both English and Indian populations. The variable structure was established by means of scalogram analysis (Guttman, 1950). The analysis is designed to examine the relationships between the scale items in which a perfect scale is one in which a person who passes an item of given difficulty will also pass any other item of lesser difficulty. Conversely, an individual who fails an item of given difficulty will also fail any other item of greater difficulty.

Because thinking stage is regarded as a partial function of age, the variable was transformed into a thinking stage quotient by dividing the absolute thinking stage score by the respondent's age in months and multiplying by a constant so that it became a percentage figure. Thus, thinking stage is not an absolute quantity but, rather, a quotient or quantity relative to age varying from a low of zero to a high of one hundred.

X_6 READ—*Reading comprehension.* The Thorndike (*51*) reading comprehension test, corrected for guessing, was used in two ways. First, it was used to define illiteracy in order that illiterates could be eliminated from the samples. The correction for guessing formula (see footnote a to Table A.1) above allows for a score of 0.0 by random guessing. In order to permit the study of the largest possible samples, the liberal cut-off point of scores greater than one was used. This eliminated $100 - (1289/1821) \times 100 = 29.2$ percent of the India sample, and $100 - (1419/1474) \times 100 = 3.7$ percent of the England sample. Second, the test was used as the measure of the reading comprehension variable. The tests consisted of reading passages followed by multiple choice questions designed to cover a wide range of reading skills. The K-R 20 formula provided reliability coefficients in England of .887, and in India of .684. The India K-R 20 coefficient might not normally be regarded as high enough to permit useful studies of individual correlates of reading. In the present instance, however, the nonreaders (29 percent of the total) were eliminated from the India sample. By definition, reliability is the tendency toward consistency from one set of measurements to another. Undoubtedly, much of the unreliability of the reading test in India was attributable to the presence of pupils who randomly guessed at test items because of their reading disability. By eliminating mere "guesses" from the sample, it is predicted that the reliability of the test sample would approximate the median reliability of .85 for the fifteen IEA countries taking part in the reading survey. Note that the corrected reading score was transformed into a percentage figure.

X_7 thru X_{10}—*Physics, chemistry, biology, practical.* The test items and the test construction procedures of the IEA science committee are described in Comber and Keeves (*14*). The overall science test score for each child was

Table A.2
Science Test Reliabilities for England and India
(Kuder-Richardson 20)[a]

TESTS	ENGLAND[b]	INDIA[b]
Science Total	.89	.78
Physics	.72	.56
Chemistry	.70	.52
Biology	.60	.32
Practical	.68	.48

a) Source: Comber and Keeves (*14*:396)

b) In both England and India some boys were included in the samples even though they fell outside the age range (1-.0 - 14.11). These "outsiders" were eliminated from the test sample. Similarly, illiterates were eliminated. Since the eliminated pupils were likely to constitute the majority of the random guessers, it is predicted, but not demonstrated here, that some of the moderate subtest coefficients will be strengthened by their elimination from the test sample.

based on an additive combination of four subtest scores in physics, chemistry, biology, and practical work. Only about ten questions were related to each subtest area in order to limit testing time to about one hour. The result was that subtest reliabilities were on the modest side, though, the overall K-R 20 reliability coefficient in science was high enough (median value = .83) to permit useful correlates of it. The relevant science test reliabilities for India and England are provided in Table A.2. All subtest science scores were converted into percentages.

(2) *Frequency Distributions*

The dispersion statistics for the ten variables are presented in Table A.3.

Table A.3

Means, Standard Deviations, Kurtosis, Skewness, Minimum and Maximum Scores, Case Base, and Missing Data for Variables Included in the General Model of the Structure of Scholastic Performance in England and India (Boys Only)[a]

VARIBLE	$\bar{X}$	SD	Kurtosis	Skewness	Minimum	Maximum	Case Base	Missing Data%
X_1 FATHOCC	2.8	1.8	-0.02	0.86	0.0	7.0	1467	1.0
	3.9	1.7	0.5	1.19	0.0	9.0	1208	8.8
X_2 PARED	6.5	1.3	1.29	-0.23	2.0	10.0	1412	4.7
	3.8	2.0	0.92	1.23	2.0	10.0	1288	2.7
X_3 SIBSZ	3.2	1.3	-1.2	0.09	1.0	5.0	1473	0.6
	4.2	1.1	0.90	-1.32	1.0	5.0	1294	2.3
X_4 VOCAB*	37.0	23.4	-0.15	-0.26	-24.7	100.0	1475	0.5
	18.9	22.0	0.25	0.54	-24.7	95.0	1271	4.0
X_5 THINK*	52.6	22.0	-0.51	0.00	0.0	96.6	1247	15.8
	42.3	21.8	-0.35	0.09	0.0	99.5	1091	17.6
X_6 READ*	48.0	20.6	-0.75	-0.18	2.5	94.8	1419	4.2
	16.3	11.7	1.00	1.15	2.5	59.0	1289	2.6
X_7 PHYSICS*	40.3	21.6	-0.39	0.30	-17.7	100.00	1421	4.1
	18.2	16.8	0.79	0.70	-20.0	84.1	1277	3.5
X_8 CHEMISTRY*	22.3	21.3	0.38	0.70	-24.7	100.00	1420	4.2
	10.3	16.4	1.52	0.95	-24.7	81.6	1264	4.5
X_9 BIOLOGY*	27.6	18.9	0.00	0.34	-17.9	93.7	1421	4.1
	12.0	13.4	0.52	0.48	-24.7	67.4	1277	3.5
X_{10} PRACTICAL*	24.1	21.9	-0.12	0.61	-18.5	100.0	1408	5.0
	6.4	14.4	0.84	0.86	-24.5	62.5	1221	7.8
X_{11} SCIENCE[b]*	28.8	17.8	0.09	0.70	-11.5	87.5	1421	4.1
	11.7	11.1	2.26	1.13	-12.4	62.9	1277	3.5

a) Statistics for England on the upper line; statistics for India on the bottom line, in each instance.

b) SCIENCE = X7 + X8 + X9 + X10. The raw science score corrected for guessing was transformed into a percentage figure.

* Starred variables are reported as percentages.

c) Minus quantities are possible because raw scores were corrected for guessing.

TECHNICAL APPENDIX B: STATISTICAL RESULTS

Five sets of data are presented in Appendix B. First, the zero-order correlations between the variables in the model of the structure of scholastic performance are presented in Table B.1. Second, the correlations are used to generate the structural coefficients for a fully-identified model by ordinary least squares. These comparisons are presented in Table B.2. Third, the total causal effects of predicted variables are presented in Table B.3., followed by a summary Table (B.4.) in which the total causal effects are ranked for ease of reference. Tables B.5. and B.6. relate to the interpretation of residual scores. Finally, using India data from Table B.2., a respecified final form path model is presented.

Figure B.1 Respecified Path Model of the Structure of Natural Science Performances for Fourteen-Year-Old Boys in India.[a]

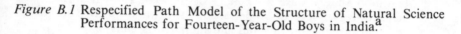
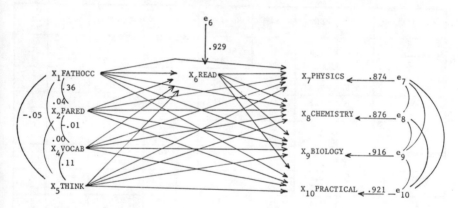

[a] Path coefficient approximations may be obtained from Table B.2. The correlations between the residuals may be obtained from Table B.5. The model differs from the conceptual model (Figure 1.1.) in that the SIBZ(X_3) variable has been dropped and the VOCAB (X_4) and THINK (X_5) variables have been made into source variables.

Table B.1
Correlations, Means, Standard Deviations, and Case Base of Variables in the Model of the Structure of Scholastic for England and India[a]

VARIABLES	X_1	X_2	X_3	X_4	X_5	X_6	X_7	X_8	X_9	X_{10}	X_{11}	$\bar{X}$	SD	CASES
X_1 FATHOCC		.242	-.171	.314	.129	.295	.279	.235	.249	.272	.307	2.83	1.8	1467
X_2 PARED	.360		-.081	.122	.074	.129	.124	.138	.161	.162	.171	6.5	1.3	1412
X_3 S1BS2	.041	-.025		-.182	-.091	-.166	-.165	-.145	-.163	-.184	-.195	3.2	1.3	1473
X_4 VOCAB	.041	-.010	.023		.287	.647	.511	.503	.479	.509	.591	37.0	23.4	1475
X_5 THINK	-.052	.000	-.004	.107		.365	.398	.406	.448	.358	.469	52.6	22.0	1247
X_6 READ	.012	.031	.033	.364	.087		.638	.592	.585	.610	.716	48.0	20.6	1419
X_7 PHYSICS	.138	.103	-.001	.345	.186	.386		.642	.588	.681	.874	40.3	21.6	1421
X_8 CHEMISTRY	.101	.122	.009	.290	.224	.400	.471		.569	.666	.847	22.3	21.3	1420
X_9 BIOLOGY	.041	.050	.025	.297	.235	.275	.338	.240		.591	.791	27.6	18.9	1421
X_{10} PRACTICAL	.120	.092	.025	.281	.066	.329	.403	.439	.266		.873	24.1	21.9	1408
X_{11} SCIENCE	.140	.132	.019	.421	.244	.481	.808	.755	.596	.720		28.8	17.8	1421
$\bar{X}$	3.9	3.8	4.2	18.9	42.3	16.3	18.2	10.3	12.0	6.4	11.7			
SD	1.7	2.0	1.1	22.0	21.8	11.7	16.8	16.4	13.4	14.4	11.1			
CASES	1208	1288	1294	1271	1091	1289	1277	1264	1277	1221	1277			

[a]English data above the diagonal; India data below the diagonal.

Table B.2

England/India Comparisons of the Structural Coefficients for the Fully Identified Model of Scholastic Performance by Ordinary Least Squares: I) Regression Coefficients, II) Path Coefficients, III) Standard Errors[a]

DEPENDENT VARIABLES

Independent Variables	VOCAB(X4) I	II	III	THINK(X5) I	II	III	READ(X6) I	II	III	PHYSICS(X7) I	II	III	CHEMISTRY(X8) I	II	III	BIOLOGY(X9) I	II	III	PRACTICAL(X10) I	II	III	SCIENCE(X11) I	II	III
X1 FATHOCC	3.745	.281	.349	.400	.032	.377	.990	.084	.271	.850	.069	.287	.293	.024	.294	.433	.040	.258	.681	.054	.301	.585	.058	.205
	.656	.051	.408	-.839	-.065	.434	-.106	-.015	.218	1.125	.114	.296	.665	.069	.290	.207	.026	.247	.670	.079	.267	.677	.103	.180
X2 PARED	-.761	.043	.459	.515	.031	.477	.379	.024	.343	.254	.015	.361	.706	.044	.370	.907	.064	.324	.986	.059	.377	.703	.052	.257
	-.311	-.028	.351	.271	.025	.374	.241	.041	.188	.470	.055	.254	.735	.088	.249	.257	.038	.212	.425	.058	.230	.486	.086	.154
X3 SIBSZ	-2.359	-.130	.463	-.586	-.034	.485	-.503	-.031	.349	-.593	-.035	.368	-.370	-.022	.376	-.598	-.041	.330	-.978	-.057	.385	-.652	-.047	.262
	.411	.020	.602	-.064	-.003	.640	.293	.027	.321	-.283	-.018	.435	-.066	-.004	.426	.185	.015	.363	.139	.010	.393	-.002	.000	.264
X4 VOCAB				.252	.267	.028	.493	.558	.021	.123	.133	.026	.161	.177	.027	.107	.132	.024	.151	.161	.028	.136	.178	.019
				.109	.110	.031	.190	.360	.016	.167	.220	.023	.112	.150	.022	.127	.209	.019	.118	.181	.021	.133	.264	.014
X5 THINK							.177	.189	.021	.177	.180	.023	.200	.206	.023	.222	.259	.020	.141	.141	.024	.182	.225	.016
							.026	.048	.016	.110	.143	.022	.138	.183	.021	.122	.199	.018	.019	.029	.020	.097	.190	.013
X6 READ										.480	.458	.030	.398	.386	.031	.345	.378	.027	.448	.421	.032	.421	.487	.022
										.419	.291	.043	.457	.325	.042	.205	.179	.036	.318	.257	.039	.348	.365	.026
Residual	.939			.956			.733			.736			.764			.757			.759			.636		
	.998			.992			.929			.874			.876			.916			.921			.784		
Constant	28.938			40.678			16.730			1.193			-17.650			-9.821			-15.697			-10.217		
	15.853			42.744			9.848			-1.472			-10.265			-1.437			-6.650			-5.090		
100R²	11.733			8.626			46.334			45.893			41.609			42.696			42.453			59.520		
	.003			1.524			13.725			23.642			23.255			16.162			15.165			35.875		

[a] Statistics for England on the upper line; statistics for India on lower line, in each instance.

Table B.3
Total Causal Effects of Predictor Variables for Scholastic Performances in the Natural Sciences: England/India Comparisons for Male Pupils[a]

(1) Independent Variables	(2) Dependent Variables	(3) Total Indirect Effects Through Intervening Variables	(4) Direct Effect	(5) Total Causal Effect
X_1 FATHOCC	X_4 VOCAB	– –	.281 .051	.281 .051
	X_5 THINK	.075 .006	.032 -.065	.107 -.059
	X_6 READ	.177 .015	.084 -.015	.261 .000
	X_7 PHYSICS	.175 .003	.069 .114	.244 .117
	X_8 CHEMISTRY	.171 -.008	.024 .069	.195 .061
	X_9 BIOLOGY	.167 -.004	.040 .026	.207 .022
	X_{10} PRACTICAL	.170 .003	.054 .079	.224 .082
	X_{11} SCIENCE	.201 .003	.058 .103	.259 .106

[a] Statistics for England on the upper line; statistics for India on lower line, in each instance.

(1)	(2)	(3)	(4)	(5)
X_2PARED	X_4VOCAB	– –	.043 -.028	<u>.043</u> <u>-.028</u>
	X_5THINK	.011 .003	.031 .025	<u>.042</u> <u>.028</u>
	X_6READ	.032 .011	.024 .041	.056 .052
	X_7PHYSICS	.039 .025	.015 .055	.054 .080
	X_8CHEMISTRY	.038 .025	.044 .088	.082 .113
	X_9BIOLOGY	.038 .019	.064 .038	.102 .057
	X_{10}PRACTICAL	.036 .019	.059 .058	.095 .077
	X_{11}SCIENCE	.045 .008	.052 .086	.097 .094
X_3S1BS2	X_4VOCAB	– –	-.130 .020	-.130 <u>.020</u>
	X_5THINK	-.035 .002	-.034 -.003	-.069 <u>-.001</u>
	X_6READ	-.085 .001	-.031 .027	-.116 <u>.028</u>
	X_7PHYSICS	-.111 .004	-.035 -.018	-.146 <u>-.014</u>
	X_8CHEMISTRY	-.082 .003	-.022 -.004	-.104 <u>-.001</u>
	X_9BIOLOGY	-.079 .004	-.041 .015	-.120 <u>.019</u>
	X_{10}PRACTICAL	-.080 .004	-.057 .010	-.137 <u>.014</u>
	X_{11}SCIENCE	-.092 .012	-.047 .000	-.139 <u>.012</u>

(1)	(2)	(3)	(4)	(5)
X_4VOCAB	X_5THINK	– –	.267 .110	.267 .110
	X_6READ	.050 .005	.558 .360	.608 .365
	X_7PHYSICS	.327 .122	.133 .220	.460 .342
	X_8CHEMISTRY	.290 .139	.177 .150	.467 .289
	X_9BIOLOGY	.299 .087	.132 .209	.431 .296
	X_{10}PRACTICAL	.294 .096	.161 .181	.455 .277
	X_{11}SCIENCE	.367 .154	.178 .264	.545 .418
X_5THINK	X_6READ	– –	.189 .048	.189 .048
	X_7PHYSICS	.087 .014	.180 .143	.267 .157
	X_8CHEMISTRY	.073 .016	.206 .183	.279 .199
	X_9BIOLOGY	.071 .009	.259 .199	.330 .208
	X_{10}PRACTICAL	.080 .012	.141 .029	.221 .041
	X_{11}SCIENCE	.092 .017	.225 .190	.317 .207
X_6READ	X_7PHYSICS	– –	.458 .291	.458 .291
	X_8CHEMISTRY	– –	.386 .325	.386 .325
	X_9BIOLOGY	– –	.378 .179	.378 .179
	X_{10}PRACTICAL	– –	.421 .257	.421 .257
	X_{11}SCIENCE	– –	.487 .365	.487 .365

Table B.4

Within-Country Rank Ordering of Total Causal Effects of Predictor Variables on Endogenous Variables: England/India Comparisons[a]

Predictor	VOCAB	THINK	READ	PHYSICS	CHEMISTRY	BIOLOGY	PRACTICAL	SCIENCE
				R A N K O R D E R				
X_1 FATHOCC	1 .281	2 .107	2 .261	4 .244	4 .195	4 .207	3 .224	4 .259
	1 .051	2 -.059	5 .000	4 .117	5 .061	5 .022	3 .082	4 .106
X_2 PARED	3 .043	4 .042	5 .056	6 .054	6 .082	6 .102	6 .095	6 .097
	2 -.028	3 .028	2 .052	5 .080	4 .113	4 .057	6 .007	5 .094
X_3 S1BS2	2 -.130	3 -.069	4 -.116	5 -.146	5 -.104	5 -.120	5 -.137	5 -.139
	3 .020	4 -.001	4 .028	6 -.014	6 -.001	6 .019	5 .014	6 .012
X_4 VOCAB		1 .267	1 .608	1 .460	1 .467	1 .431	1 .455	1 .545
		1 .110	1 .365	1 .342	2 .289	1 .296	1 .277	1 .418
X_5 THINK			3 .189	3 .267	3 .279	3 .330	4 .221	3 .317
			3 .048	3 .157	3 .199	2 .208	4 .041	3 .207
X_6 READ				2 .458	2 .386	2 .378	2 .421	2 .487
				2 .291	1 .325	3 .179	2 .257	2 .365

[a] The total causal effects are to the right of the rank order figures in each column. Note that these total causal effects are relative not absolute totals. The underlined TCE's are considered to be of negligible substantive significance.

Correlations between the Residuals of the Natural Science Outcomes: India/ England Comparisons[a]

Variable		X_7	X_8	X_9	X_{10}
X_7 PHYSICS	E		.370	.272	.435
	I		.315	.189	.272
X_8 CHEMISTRY	E	.642		.259	.430
	I	.471		.069	.324
X_9 BIOLOGY	E	.588	.569		.303
	I	.338	.240		.152
X_{10} PRACTICAL	E	.681	.666	.591	
	I	.403	.439	.266	

[a] Partial correlations controlling for all antecedent variables above the diagonal; zero-order relationships below the diagonal. Statistics for England on upper line and for India on the lower line.

Table B.6
Proportion of Covariance between Natural Science Performances Accounted for by the Antecedent Variables[a]

Variable		X_7	X_8	X_9	X_{10}
X_7 PHYSICS	E		.424	.537	.361
	I		.331	.441	.325
X_8 CHEMISTRY	E	–		.545	.354
	I	–		.754	.262
X_9 BIOLOGY	E	–	–		.487
	I	–	–		.428
X_{10} PRACTICAL	E	–	–	–	
	I	–	–	–	

[a] Statistics for England on upper line and for India on lower line. Median proportions: England = .455; India = .379.

References

1. Athey, Irene J. "Synthesis of Papers on Language Development and Reading," in F.B. David (Ed.), *The Literature of Research in Reading with Emphasis on Models.* New Brunswick, New Jersey: Graduate School of Education, Rutgers University, 1971.
2. Bergling, Kurt. *The Development of Hypothetico-Deductive Thinking in Children.* New York: Wiley (Halstead Press), 1974.
3. Blalock, Hubert M., Jr. *Causal Models in the Social Sciences.* Chicago: Aldine Atherton, 1971.
4. Bloom, Benjamin S. *Cross-National Study of Educational Attainment: Stage One of the IEA Investigation in Six Subject Areas.* Washington, D.C.: Department of Health, Education and Welfare, Office of Education. Final Report Project No. 6-2527, Grant No. HEW-OEG-3-6-062527-2226, 1969.
5. Bloomfield, Leonard, and C. Barnhart. *Let's Read: A Linguistic Approach.* Detroit: Wayne State University Press, 1961.
6. Brodbeck, M. "Models, Meaning, and Theories," in L. Gross (Ed.), *Symposium on Sociological Theory.* New York: Harper and Row, 1959.
7. Bulcock, Jeffrey W. *Achievement in Mother Tongue Literature.* Report No. 5, Institute for the Study of International Problems in Education, University of Stockholm, 1974.
8. Bulcock, Jeffrey W. *Toward a General Model of the Structure of Scholastic Performance.* Report No. 12, Institute for the Study of International Problems in Education, University of Stockholm, 1976.
9. Bulcock, Jeffrey W., and Mona J. Beebe. *Reading in the Structure of Scholastic Performance.* Report No. 13, Institute for the Study of International Problems in Education, University of Stockholm, Sweden, 1976.
10. Bulcock, Jeffrey W., and Jeremy D. Finn. "Explaining School Performance in Literature: Some Strategies of Causal Analysis," *Scandinavian Journal of Educational Research*, 19 (1975), 75-110.
11. Carroll, John B. "The Nature of the Reading Process," in H. S. Singer and R. B. Ruddell (Eds.), *Theoretical Models and Processes of Reading,* Second Edition. Newark, Delaware: International Reading Association, 1976.
12. Carroll, John B. *Learning form Verbal Discourse in Educational Media: A Review of the Literature.* U.S.O.E. Final Report, Project No. 7-1069. Princeton, New Jersey: Educational Testing Service, 1971.
13. Carroll, John B. *French as a Foreign Language in Seven Countries.* Stockholm: Almqvist and Wiksell, 1975.
14. Comber, L. C., and John P. Keeves. *Science Education in Nineteen Countries.* Stockholm: Almqvist and Wiksell, 1973.
15. Day, David E. "Language Instruction for Young Children: What Ten Years of Confusion Has Taught Us," *Interchange*, 5 (1974), 59-72.
16. Downing, John. *Comparative Reading: Cross-National Studies on Behavior and Processes in Reading and Writing.* New York: Macmillan, 1973.
17. Duncan, Otis D. "Path Analysis: Sociological Examples," *American Journal of Sociology*, 72 (1966), 1-16.
18. Duncan, Otis D. *Introduction to Structural Equation Models.* New York: Academic Press, 1975.

19. Finn, Jeremy D., and Ingrid Mattsson. *Multivariate Analysis in Educational Research: Some Applications*. Report No. 7, Institute for the Study of International Problems in Education, University of Stockholm, Sweden, 1974.
20. Finney, J. "Indirect Effects in Path Analysis," *Sociological Methods and Research*, 1 (1972), 175-186.
21. Fries, Charles C. *Linguistics and Reading*. New York: Holt, Rinehart, 1962.
22. Goodman, Kenneth S. "Reading: A Psycholinguistic Guessing Game," in H. S. Singer and R. B. Ruddell (Eds.), *Theoretical Models and Processes of Reading*, Second Edition. Newark, Delaware: International Reading Association, 1976. (Originally published in *Journal of the Reading Specialist*, 6 (1967), 126-135.)
23. Goodman, Kenneth S. "Analysis of Oral Reading Miscues: Applied Psycholinguistics," *Reading Research Quarterly*, 5 (1969), 9-30.
24. Goodman, Kenneth S. "The Reading Process: Theory and Practice." in R. E. Hodges and E. H. Rudorf (Eds.), *Language and Leaning to Read: What Teachers Ought to Know About Language*. Boston: Houghton Mifflin, 1972.
25. Goodman, Kenenth S., and Carolyn L. Burke. *Study of Oral Reading Miscues that Result in Grammatical Retransformations*. U.S.O.E. Final Report, Project No. 7-E-219. Washington, D.C: U.S. Department of Health, Education and Welfare, 1969, Eric ED039101.
26. Goodman, Yetta M. *Longitudinal Study of Children's Oral Reading Behavior*. U.S.O.E. Final Report, Project No. 9-E-062. Washington, D.C.: Department of Health, Education and Welfare, 1971.
27. Goodman, Yetta M., and Carolyn L. Burke. *Reading Miscue Inventory*. New York: Macmillan, 1972.
28. Gray, William S. *The Teaching of Reading and Writing*. Paris: Unesco, 1956.
29. Green, Bert F. "Attitude Measurement," in G. Lindzey (Ed.), *Handbook of Social Psychology*. Reading, Massachusetts: Addision-Wesley, 1954, 335-369.
30. Hauser, Robert M. *Socioeconomic Background and Educational Performance*. The Arnold Rose Monograph Series in Sociology. Washington, D.C.: American Sociological Association, 1971.
31. Hochberg, J. "Components of Literacy: Speculations and Exploratory Research," in H. Levin and J. P. Williams (Eds.), *Basic Studies on Reading*. New York: Basic Books, 1970.
32. Hochberg, Julian, and Virginia Brooks. "Reading As an International Behavior," in H. S. Singer and R. B. Ruddell (Eds.), *Theoretical Models and Processes of Reading*, Second Edition. Newark, Delaware: International Reading Association, 1976.
33. Husen, Torsten (Ed.). *International Study of Achievement in Mathematics*, Volumes 1 and 2. New York: Wiley, 1967.
34. Kolers, Paul A. "Reading is Only Incidentally Visual," in K. Goodman and J. Fleming (Eds.), *Psycholinguistics and the Teaching of Reading*. Newark, Delaware: International Reading Association, 1969.
35. Lefevre, Carl A. *Linguistics and the Teaching of Reading*. New York: McGraw-Hill, 1964.
36. Lewis, E. G., and Carolyn Massad. *English as a Foreign Langauge in Ten Countries: An Empirical Study*. Stockholm: Almqvist and Wiksell, 1976.
37. Passow, A. H., E. J. Noah, and M. Eckstein. *The National Case Study: An Empirical Study*. Stockholm: Almqvist and Wiksell, 1976.

38. Peaker, Gilbert F. *An Empirical Study of Education in Twenty-One Countries: A Technical Report.* Stockholm: Almqvist and Wiksell, 1976.
39. Pflaum, Susanna W. *The Development of Language and Reading in the Young Child.* Columbus, Ohio: Charles E. Merrill, 1974.
40. Piaget, Jean. "The Attainment of Invariants and Reversible Operations in the Development of Thinking," *Social Research*, 30 (1963), 283-299.
41. Piaget, Jean. "Autobiography," in S. F. Campbell (Ed.), *Piaget Sampler.* New York: Wiley, 1976. (Originally published in *Cahiers Vilfred Pareto*, 10 (1966), translated by S. F. Campbell and E. Rutschi-Herrmann.)
42. Purves, Alan C. *Literature Education in Ten Countries.* Stockholm: Almqvist and Wiksell, 1973.
43. Rawson, Hildred. "A Study of the Relationships and Development of Reading and Cognition," unpublished doctoral dissertation, University of Alberta, 1969.
44. Rehberg, Richard A., and Evelyn Rosenthal. *Social Class and Merit in High School: A Multistudy Analysis.* Binghamton: Center for Comparative Political Research, State University of New York, 1975.
45. Russell, David H. *Children Learn to Read.* New York: Ginn, 1961.
46. Sinclair-De-Zwart, H. A. "A Possible Theory of Language Acquisition Within the General Framework of Piaget's Developmental Theory," in P. Adams (Ed.), *Language in Thinking.* Baltimore, Maryland: Penguin, 1972, 364-373.
47. Smith, Frank. *Understanding Reading.* Toronto: Holt, Rinehart and Winston, 1971.
48. Smith, Frank. "Decoding: The Great Fallacy," in F. Smith (Ed.), *Psycholinguistics and Reading.* Toronto: Holt, Rinehart and Winston, 1973.
49. Smith, Frank. *Comprehension and Learning.* Toronto: Holt, Rinehart and Winston, 1975.
50. Thorndike, Edward L. "Reading as Reasoning: A Study of Mistakes in Paragraph Reading," *Journal of Educational Psychology,* 8 (June 1917), 323-332. (Reprinted in *Reading Research Quarterly*, 6 (1971), 425-448.)
51. Thorndike, Robert L. *Reading Comprehension Education in Fifteen Countries.* Stockholm: Almqvist and Wiksell, 1973a.
52. Thorndike, Robert L. "The Relation of School Achievements to the Differences in the Backgrounds of Children," paper presented at the IEA Conference on Educational Achievement, Harvard University, 1973b.
53. Thorndike, Robert L. "Reading as Reasoning," *Reading Research Quarterly,* 9 (1973-1974), 135-147.
54. Torney, Judith V., A. N. Oppenhem, and R. F. Farnen. *Civic Education in Ten Countries: An Empirical Study.* Almqvist and Wiksell, Stockholm, 1975.
55. Vygotsky, Lev S. *Thought and Language.* Cambridge, Massachusetts: MIT Press, 1962.
56. Walker, D. A. *The IEA Six-Subject Survey: An Empirical Study of Education in Twenty-One Countries.* Stockholm: Almqvist and Wiksell, 1976.
57. Wardhaugh, R. *Reading: A Linguistic Perspective.* New York: Harcourt Brace Jovanovich, 1969.
58. Wright, Sewell. "The Method of Path Coefficients," *Annals of Mathematical Statistics,* 5 (1934), 161-215.

59. Williams, Trevor H. "Educational Aspirations: Longitudinal Evidence on Their Development in Canadian Youth," *Sociology of Education*, 45 (Spring 1972), 107-133.
60. Zajonc, R. B. "Family Configuration and Intelligence," *Science*, 192 (April 1976), 192-227.
61. Zajonc, R. B., and Gregory B. Markus. "Intellectual Environment and Intelligence," *Psychological Review*, 82 (1975).

Cloze Procedure and Comprehension: An Exploratory Study Across Three Languages

Hans U. Grundin
Teachers College of Linköping
Linköping, Sweden

Brother Leonard Courtney
University of British Columbia
Vancouver, British Columbia, Canada

Judith Langer
East Meadow, New York, Public Schools
United States of America

Robert Pehrsson
Lexington School for the Deaf
Flushing, New York
United States of America

H. Alan Robinson
Hofstra University
Hempstead, New York
United States of America

Takahiko Sakamoto
Noma Institute of Educational Research
Tokyo, Japan

PURPOSES

The purposes of the exploratory study reported here were formulated as follows at an early stage of its planning.

- To assess the effectiveness of the cloze technique as a measure of comprehension across three languages: English, Japanese, and Swedish;
- To ascertain the similarities and differences of cloze responses in relation to various cultural and linguistic backgrounds;

- To discover if the cloze technique tends to measure responses to "breaks in the flow of language" or overall understanding of the passage.

As is often the case in exploratory research, our experiences during the planning and pilot work stages provided new insights, which made it necessry to adjust or limit the scope of the study. We will not try to describe here exactly what kind of adjustments and limitations were thought necessary, since we believe that the discussion of results contained in this report will indicate clearly to what extent the study fulfilled the purposes as stated above.

GENERAL DESIGN OF THE STUDY

Various aspects of the empirical study (texts, translations, student samples, testing procedures, scoring) are discussed in some detail in later sections of this report. Here we present a brief account of the general design.

One prose passage containing 250-300 words was selected in each of the three languages and was translated into the other two languages. In this way, we attempted to ensure that the set of texts used in the study was neither culturally nor linguistically biased in favor of any national sample of children. The English versions of the passages are included at the end of this chapter. The passages are named 'Wolf-man" (English original) "Bats" (Japanese original), and "Diviner" (Swedish original).

For each of the nine text versions (three in each language), a cloze test following recognized procedures was prepared by means of deletion of every fifth word. A global question concerning the overall meaning of the passage was determined on the basis of pilot studies in Vancouver, Canada. This question was translated into Japanese and Swedish:

"In at least three sentences, tell what is the main idea of the story."

In each participating country, a sample of approximately 150 children in grade five (in Sweden grades four and five, due to difference in school entrance age) constituted the subjects of the study. All the children were native speakers of the national language in question, and were pupils in normal classes, i.e., excluding pupils with reading or learning disability.

Each national sample of children was given a short cloze test practice session, then the three cloze tests based on the passages in their own language, followed by the global question relating to each passage. Before answering the global question (but after completing the cloze test), the children were given the opportunity to read the complete text, without the deletions in the cloze test. They were also allowed to refer back to the complete text of the passage during their answering of the global question. The purpose of this feature was two-fold: 1) to ensure that children were not handicapped by inability to fill in the deletions in the cloze test when they tried to determine the main ideas; and 2) to avoid making performance on the global comprehension task unduly dependent upon the child's memory of the passage read.

One session was devoted to each passage (cloze test, reading of complete text, and answering of global question), and the children were allowed up to 35 minutes on each session. Children could start individually with the global task as soon as they had finished the cloze test. The order of presentation of the three passages was rotated within each national sample.

PILOT STUDY

To assess the methodology of the proposed international study, a pilot study was conducted in Vancouver during October and November 1974. Its objectives were to establish testing procedures, particularly to determine time necessary to do the cloze passage and the exact phrasing of the global question to elicit maximum response from subjects.

The cloze passage used was the English original, "Wolfman." Normal cloze procedures were followed. Two graduate assistants administered the cloze passage and the various global questions to 110 fifth grade pupils in six different Vancouver city schools. Testing groups varied from 10 to 15 pupils. A committee of judges designed, modified, and evaluated the various steps in development, administration, and assessment. A criterion answer, which reduced responses to ten individual points within the passage, was constructed for each global question.

PASSAGES, TRANSLATIONS, AND CLOZE TESTS

The passages used in the study were selected by three different members of the research team—one American, one Japanese, and one Swedish. Each chose a text in his own language on the basis of the following main criteria for selection:

- length of passage (250-300 words)
- difficulty level (suitable for the average reader in grade five)
- nature of content (mainly factual but dealing with unusual or puzzling events or phenomena)
- structure of passage (it should contain a "finished," although brief and possibly very simplified, treatment of its topic, and not an excerpt from a longer text).

Each passage was then translated into the other two languages. All translations were initially made by native speakers of the language *from* which a passage should be translated, and later checked for suitability for grade five (vocabulary, syntx, etc.) by native speakers of the language *into* which the passage had been translated. The aim of both the translations and the revisions of translations was to make the translated passages as natural and genuine in terms of language as the original passage, without changing the content. Revisions of translations also had the aim of ensuring that the translated passages were similar to the original passage in difficulty (or readability) level.

As previously indicated, the cloze tests were prepared according to established principles. Since the length of the passages varied, this provided different numbers of deletions in different tests, as shown below.

| | Number of deletions in: | | |
Passage	English version	Japanese version	Swedish version
"Bats"	51	71	51
"Diviner"	57	74	50
"Wolfman"	50	64	50
Total	158	209	151

Reliability coefficients for the various passages were computed for each national sample by means of Kuder-Richardson's formula 21. The average reliability (KR21) for passages in each of the three languages is 0.73 for English, 0.65 for Japanese, and 0.80 for Swedish.

STUDENT SAMPLES

The different national samples are described in the table below. The most notable differences in the characteristics included concern the Japanese sample as compared to the others. The proportion of boys is very low in the Japanese sample—only 27 percent against 44 to 57 percent in the other samples. And the Japanese children in grade five are considerably older than comparable groups in Canada and the United States (grade five) or in Sweden (grade four).

All the national samples are from urban or suburban areas, and are believed to represent a cross section of socioeconomic groups, while avoiding—as planned—both very low and very high socioeconomic groups.

Characteristic	Canada gr. 5	USA gr. 5	Japan gr. 5	Sweden gr. 4	Sweden gr. 5
Number of children[1]	131	188	129	132	119
Percentage boys	44	57	27	51	51
Median age	10.0	10.1	10.8	10.0	11.0
Number of classes	—[2]	8	4	5	5
Average class size[3]	—	23	32	29	27
Number of schools	4	1	1	2	2

1) Number of children with complete set of data. Actual number of children in participating classes usually somewhat larger.
2) The Canadian sample consisted of selected groups of average readers from a fairly large number of classes. This was in agreement with the initial sampling plan for the study, which was later discussed for the other national samples.
3) Based on the total number of children in the classes, including those who were absent from one or more testing sessions.

It has not been possible, within the context of this study, to determine to what extent the various national samples are representative of the population of grade five (or grades four and five) children in each country. Samples of children from only a handful of classes can, of course, never be truly representative of nationwide variety. It seems reasonable to believe, however, that the subjects of this study are samples of average or normal children at this particular age level in urban or suburban areas of British Columbia (Canada), New York/New York State (USA), Japan, and Sweden.

TESTING PROCEDURES

The testing involved in this study was carried out in October and November 1975. Each class was tested separately, as one group, during three sessions time-tabled at three different days during a two-week period.

The children in the United States were tested by their own classroom teachers, who had been given training and instructions prior to the first session. All the other national samples were tested by testers who were specially engaged for this task, which means (among other things) that the tests were administered by adults whom the children did not know beforehand.

SCORING OF THE TESTS

Cloze test scores

All cloze tests were scored according to the conventional number right method, i.e., one point is given for each completion which agrees with the word deleted from the original text (disregarding spelling errors). This means that the child had to fill in not only the right word but also its correct grammatical form (number and case for nouns, tense for verbs), before getting credit for the response.

Global task scores

Children's replies to the global question had to be evaluated by means of content analysis. That is, it had to be decided for each reply to what extent it contained formulations which were acceptable synonyms of a set of model formulations of basic ideas or concepts. Such analysis necessarily involves an element of subjectivity, since the exact content of a written reply to a question often cannot be determined without ambiguity. This subjectivity was minimized as two independent judges were engaged in the analysis.

In order to arrive at a structured and fairly objective scoring system, a set of three basic ideas was defined for each passage.

"Bats"

1. Bats are able to fly in the darkness without hitting anything.
2. They use their ears rather than their eyes to keep from hitting things.
3. They hear echoes from the high-pitched sounds they make.

"Diviner"

1. Diviners search for underground water.
2. They use divining rods to locate the spots where wells can be drilled.
3. Although the diviner is often right, how he does it is still a mystery.

"Wolfman"

1. Violent acts increase during the full moon.
2. The moon causes the waters of the earth to change.
3. Since our bodies are made up mostly of water, the full moon may cause changes in human behaviour.

Scoring procedure

The scoring of cloze tests and global question replies was done separately for each national sample in the country concerned. There is, strictly speaking, no way of determining whether the scoring rules were interpreted in exactly the same way for each national sample. However, the problems involved, particularly in scoring the global replies, had been discussed in great detail by members of the research team representing different language areas. We are, therefore, confident that the scoring was done according to the same basic principles in all four countries concerned.

Within each country the scoring was carried out by members of the research team or by a small group of assistants closely supervised by a member of the research team. Global question replies were scored by at least two persons, and the scores included in the data analysis are agreed upon by both scorers—if necessary after adjudication.

Grundin and others

ON CLOZE RESULTS ACROSS LANGUAGES

The results of the study seem to indicate that there is variation between languages as well as variation between texts and interactions between language and text, in the sense that when a given content is rendered in different languages the resulting cloze tests do not have the same level of difficulty.

The variation between languages consists mainly in a higher overall cloze percentage for Japanese children (52 percent) than for English speaking (46 percent) or Swedish speaking (44 percent). There seem to be several possible, although not necessarily plausible, explanations for this:

- *Japanese children are better readers* than Canadian, Swedish, or American children at the corresponding grade/age level. Whether this explanation is acceptable seems almost impossible to determine, since there is no definition of reading ability which is independent of the language read. It should be pointed out in this context that the median age for the Japanese children in this study is 10.8 years, whereas it is 10.1 for the English speaking children, and 10.5 for the Swedish children. Also, the Japanese sample has a much higher proportion of girls (73 percent) than the other national samples, and girls tend to do better on reading tests than boys.

- *The Japanese language is easier to read, has higher redundancy,* than the other two languages. On the surface, this seems plausible. The explanation rests, however, on the assumption that the average reading ability is the same in the different national samples. As the first explanation (above) shows, it is far from obvious that this is the case.

- *The Japanese text versions used are easier* that the corresponding English and Swedish versions. This explanation is reasonable only if one accepts the assumptions that the three samples of pupils have the same average reading ability and that the three languages involved are equally "easy to read" in a general sense. The second of these assumptions seems tenable but, as we have seen, the first is questionable.

What we *can* fairly safely conclude from these results is that a given cloze percentage need not have the same meaning or significance in different language areas. In fact, it is even possible that the cloze procedure does not measure exactly the same aspect of reading ability in different languages.

The effect of translation

One interesting aspect of cloze results across languages is the effect of translation from langauge to language. For each linguistic group, the study shows the mean cloze percentages for nontranslated (original) and for translated texts. The values for nontranslated texts are consistently higher than those for the translated texts: overall mean is 54 percent for nontranslated texts, compared to 44 percent for translated texts.

This seems to indicate that translation from one language to another makes a text more difficult to read. Or, to be more precise, translated texts tend to be less predictable for children aged ten and eleven years than nontranslated texts, even when efforts have been made to make the texts equivalent.

The difference in cloze percentage between translated and nontranslated texts tend to be less predictable for children aged ten and smallest for the English speaking groups (4 percent) and largest for the Swedish (almost 16 percent). Since very few texts and translators have been used in this study, it does not seem possible to tell whether this difference is accidental (e.g., due to different degrees of success in the translation efforts) or reflects some difference between the languages.

Another practical consequence of our findings about the effect of translation is that versions of cloze tests in different languages are likely to become more parallel (in terms of cloze score) if all versions are translations from a language not included in the study.

RELATION BETWEEN "CLOZE COMPREHENSION" AND "GLOBAL COMPREHENSION"

The object of our global question, following each of the cloze tasks, was to assess the children's ability to identify the main ideas in the passage presented to them. If the cloze task demands understanding mainly at the literal level (or understanding at the syntactic-semantic level of successive units of meaning), the global question should, ideally, demand understanding of larger units of meaning and of the interrelations among these units of meaning. As we shall see later, it cannot be taken for granted that the global question measures precisely what it is intended to measure. The term *global comprehension*, therefore, will be used here only as a provisional label for that kind of comprehension which is measured by means of our global question.

The correlations between cloze scores and global scores for different texts and pupil groups vary considerably. All the correlation coefficients are, however, low or moderate, ranging from 0.10 to 0.57. The total cloze-total global correlations are, on the whole, higher than the cloze-global correlations for individual texts. This is probably mainly due to the very restricted variation in global scores for the individual texts: between one-third and one-half of the English speaking and Swedish children scored 0 on each text.

For the three main experimental groups—the samples from Japan, Sweden, and the United States—the total cloze-total global correlations are fairly similar, the coefficients being 0.47, 0.45 and 0.49. Since we are interested here in "cloze reading ability" and "global reading ability," it is reasonable to correct these coefficients for the attenuation caused by lack of perfect reliability in our measures of these abilities (*12*). The corrected coefficients are 0.59, 0.57 and 0.65. We may conclude, then, that cloze comprehension and global comprehension have a common variance which is about 35 percent of the total variance.

Thus, the cloze task and the global task tap to some extent the same ability, which obviously must be some kind of reading ability— or at least an ability to "process written langauge." But the two tasks do also, and to a much larger extent, measure different aspects of thinking-language-reading ability. That the two types of tasks, cloze and global, have only about 35 percent common variance does not necessarily mean that they primarily—through the 65 percent of variance which is unique for each type of task—measure *different aspects of reading ability*. Before we can draw such a conclusion, we must convince ourselves that both types of tasks primarily measure reading ability, and not to a large degree abilities of other (although perhaps related) kinds.

It is in this context interesting to see to what extent various cloze tasks—and various global tasks—measure the same thing. Indices of this are provided by the intercorrelations among cloze scores for different texts and among global scores. These intercorrelations are quite high for the cloze scores, ranging from 0.6 to 0.8, whereas they are very low for the global scores, from 0.0 to 0.3. Even in this case correction for attentuation due to lack of reliability seemed called for, particularly since cloze scores are on the whole more reliable than global scores. The average corrected correlation between cloze scores for different texts is 0.91, while the average corrected global score intercorrelation is only 0.27.

Obviously, the different cloze tests measure to a very great extent (more than 80 percent common variance) the same ability or aspect of ability. The three global tasks, however, seem to be mainly text specific (less than 10 percent common variance), in that the ability to do weil on one of these tasks has a very low correlation with the ability to do well on the two other tasks. Another reason for the low intercorrelation among global scores may be that relatively few pupils have done well on these tasks: if many subjects lack the ability measured by two different tests, one should not expect the correlation between the test scores to be high.

In view of the findings presented here we may have to conclude that our global task and our way of scoring it have not constituted an entirely suitable test of overall understanding of passages for the children included in our study. The task itself seems to have been too difficult for some children. In addition to that, our scoring system may not have revealed all the variations in performance that exist in spite of the difficulty of the task.

Many of the ten- and eleven-year-olds in our sample do not seem to have perceived the global task as well defined. Even within each national sample of children (with the exception of the Japanese sample where global scores are high) there is apparently very little in the way of a common conception of what constitutes the "main ideas" or "main content" of a passage. There is a clear contrast here between the cloze task and the global task. Children's ability to cope with cloze tasks varies greatly, and there is probably also great variation in their understanding of the best strategy for coping with cloze tasks. But the cloze task is undoubtedly well defined for most children: they are expected to "put in words that make sense."

The most important conclusions that can be drawn from our findings concerning cloze scores and global scores in this study are:

1. The cloze task and the global task *may* differ greatly as regards the kind of ability demanded in each task, but they also appear to differ greatly in that the cloze task is perceived by many children as much better defined than the global task.

2. The kind of comprehension needed to cope with cloze tasks is a necessary but not sufficient condition for the ability to cope with the global tasks (i.e., to identify main ideas).

CONCLUSIONS

The nature of "overall understanding of a passage" can be summarized in two points:

1. The global task used in this study measures primarily the ability to identify units of meaning in a passage and to judge the relative importance of these units.

2. The criteria on which mature readers base their judgments of the relative importance of different units of meaning in a passage are probably not well understood by most children ten to eleven years of age.

The effectiveness of the cloze technique as a measure of comprehension can be summarized in the following points:

1. Cloze technique provides a valid and reliable measure of an important aspect of reading comprehension.

2. In order to do well on cloze tests, a reader must be able to utilize a great deal of the redundancy of written language that exists at several text levels: phrase, sentence, and paragraph.

3. A certain level of comprehension as measured by cloze procedure is necessary before overall understanding can develop, but the fact that a reader can do well on cloze tasks is no guarantee of overall understanding or ability to identify main ideas in passages. In many cases, systematic teaching may be needed before this higher-order ability of identifying main ideas or global understanding is developed.

References

1. Bjornsson, C. H. *Lasbarhet* (Readability). In Swedish with a summary in English. Stockholm: Liber, 1968.
2. Bormuth, J. R. "Cloze Tests as Measures of Readability and Comprehension," unpublished doctoral dissertation, Indiana University, 1962.
3. Bormuth, J. R. "Cloze as a Measure of Readability," in J. A. Figurel (Ed.), *Reading as an Intellectual Activity*, Proceedings of the International Reading Association, 8. New York: Scholastic Magazines, 1963.
4. Bormuth, J. R. "Validities of Grammatical and Semantic Classification of Cloze Test Scores," in J. A. Figurel (Ed.), *Reading and Inquiry*. Proceedings, Volume 10, 1965, 283-285. Newark, Delaware: International Reading Association.
5. Bormuth, J. R. "Readability: A New Approach," *Reading Research Quarterly,* 1 (1966) 79-132.
6. Bormuth, J. R. "Cloze Test Readability: Criterion Reference Scores," *Journal of Educational Measurement,* 5 (1968), 189-196.
7. Bormuth, J. R. "Reading Literacy: Its Definition and Assessment," *Reading Research Quarterly,* 9 (1973), 7-66.
8. David, F. B. "Fundamental Factors of Comprehension in Reading," unpublished doctoral dissertation, Harvard University, 1941.
9. Davis, F. B. "Research in Comprehension in Reading," *Reading Research Quarterly,* 3 (1968), 499-545.
10. David, F. B. "Psychometric Research on Comprehension in Reading," *Reading Research Quarterly,* 7 (1972), 628-678.
11. Gallant, R. M. "An Investigation of the Use of Cloze Tests as a Measurement of Readability of Materials for the Primary Grades," unpublished doctoral dissertation, Indiana University, 1964.
12. Guilford, J. P. *Psychometric Methods.* New York: McGraw-Hill, 1954.
13. Hafner, L. E. "Relationship of Various Measures to the Cloze," *Thirteenth Yearbook of the National Reading Conference.* Milwaukee: National Reading Conference, 1963, 135-145.
14. Holland, J. G., and F. D. Kemp. "A Measure of Programming in Teaching Matching Material," *Journal of Educational Psychology,* 56 (1965), 264-269.
15. Horton, R. J. "The Construct Validity of Cloze Procedure: An Exploratory Factor Analysis of Cloze, Paragraph Reading, and Structure-of-Intellect," doctoral dissertation, Hofstra University, 1973.
16. Hunt, K. *Differences in Grammatical Structures Written at Three Grade Levels.* Urbana, Illinois: NCTE Research Report No. 3, 1965.
17. Hunt, L. C., Jr. "Can We Measure Specific Factors Associated with Reading Comprehension?" *Journal of Educational Research,* 51 (1957), 161-172.
18. Jenkinson, M. D. "Selected Processes and Difficulties in Reading Comprehension," unpublished doctoral dissertation, University of Chicago, 1957.
19. Loman, B., and N. Jorgensen. *Manual for Analys och Beskrivning av Makrosyntagmer* (Manual for the Analysis and Description of Macrosyntagms). In Swedish with a summary in English. Lund, Sweden: Student-Litteratur, 1971.
20. Nie, N. H., et al. *SPSS—Statistical Package for the Social Sciences,* Second Edition. New York: McGraw-Hill, 1975.

21. Ramanauskas, S. "The Responsiveness of Cloze Readability Measures to Linguistic Variables Operating Over Segments of Text Longer than a Sentence," *Reading Research Quarterly*, 8 (1972), 72-91.
22. Rankin, E. F. "An Evaluation of the Cloze Procedure as a Technique for Measuring Reading Comprehension," unpublished doctoral dissertation, University of Michigan, 1957.
23. Ruddell, R. B. "An Investigation of the Effects of the Similarity of Oral and Written Patterns of Language Structure on Reading Comprehension," unpublished doctoral dissertation, Indiana University, 1963.
24. Simons, H. D. "Reading Comprehension: The Need for a New Perspective," *Reading Research Quarterly*, 6 (1971), 338-363.
25. Smith, F. *Understanding Reading: A Psycholinguistic Analysis of Reading and Learning to Read*. New York: Holt, Rinehart and Winston, 1971.
26. Spearritt, D. "Identification of Subskills of Reading Comprehension by Maximum Likelihood Factors," *Reading Research Quarterly*, 8 (1972), 92-111.
27. Taylor, W. L. "Cloze Procedure: A New Tool for Measuring Readability." *Journalism Quarterly*, 30 (1953), 415-433.
28. Thorndike, R. L. "Reading as Reasoning," *Reading Research Quarterly*, 9 (1973-1974), 135-147.
29. Wheat, T. E., and R. M. Edmond. "The Concept of Comprehension: An Analysis," *Journal of Reading*, 18 (1975), 523-527.

A Comparison of Reading Achievement among Three Racial Groups Using Standard Reading Materials

Ned Ratekin
University of Northern Iowa
Cedar Falls, Iowa
United States of America

THE PROBLEM

Attempts to solve the problem of lower reading performance among minority groups, especially Black and Chicano children, often focus on sociolinguistic factors. One central concern has been the degree of "fit" between the language and cultural experience of the child and the language and cultural content of instructional materials.

The relationship between this language "fit" and success in learning to read has resulted in two areas of application. The first is based on empirical data of the type offered by Ruddell (2) who documents a direct relationship between reading comprehension and the degree to which the reader's own language matches what he is reading. Such studies indicate a relationship closely tied to the developmental level of the child's language and thought. The application of this relationship is widely used to make sure that children are offered materials written close to their own developmental levels.

The second application is inferred from the type of research cited above and is applied straightforward to language differences of style, dialect, and grammar. This application has resulted in the preparation of instructional materials written to represent the phonological and syntactic structures of Black dialect, and to contain geographical and sociological settings relevant to the experiences of specific minority groups. Although this application seems logical, research has not verified its effectiveness. Simons (3) in a brief review of the data, and Gibson and Levin (1) in a thorough analysis of the question, have emphasized both the importance of the teacher's knowledge of these language and cultural differences, and the lack of impact made by materials especially prepared to match dialect, grammar, and cultural aspects of a child's language.

In addition to language factors, a low socioeconomic level appears as a major explanation for lower reading performance of minority groups. Since children from families in lower socioeconomic neighborhoods also tend to exhibit language differences, such as Black dialect or learning English as a second language, it has been difficult to separate these factors in conducting the research relating language structure and reading performance.

PURPOSE OF THE STUDY

An evaluation of a follow through project in a large midwestern city has provided a unique opportunity to examine the relationship of language, materials of instruction, and reading performance across three racial groups—Anglo, Black, and Chicano—from a common socioeconomic level. The purpose of this study is to compare the reading progress of these children in a program which uses the same standard materials for all children, and which has teaching staff prepared to understand and accept language differences among children.

If ability to progress in reading is related to the language fit between children and materials, then using identical materials is expected to result in a real difference in average reading performance among the three groups. If the sociolinguistic nature of the material is not a crucial factor, then no differences should be found. The specific hypothesis tested in this study is:

> There is no difference in reading performance among groups of children having different language characteristics who learn to read from identical materials when those children come from the same socioeconomic level.

THE POPULATION

This study compares reading test scores from children in grades one through three in an innercity elementary school. The school is a neighborhood attendance center; no children are bused into or out of the area. For several years the neighborhood has been composed of approximately equal numbers of Anglo, Black, and Chicano families. The families from all three racial groups are classified in the lower socioeconomic level according to standards of income, housing, and education. It is assumed, for this study, that the factor of socioeconomic level as an explanation for differences among races in reading achievement has been removed.

The speech of the Black children is characterized by the dialectic qualities associated with innercity Black language. The Chicano children vary in their use of and dependency on Spanish. A few children who know little or no English enter the school each year, but the majority of Chicano families are long standing members of the community and are bilingual. Spanish is widely used in the homes, in the community, and in the school.

Reading instruction in this program is carried out through the Houghton Mifflin basal reading series and through basic skills materials in a learning center. In addition to receiving classroom instruction in reading, the children attend a learning center each day where they work individually and in small groups in basic skill activities. Materials used provide for learning through a variety of sound and projection media, letter and word card manipulation materials, and trade books. Children are assigned tasks according to basic skill needs with an emphasis on word attack activities. Instruction in the two classrooms at each level is provided by a teacher and a teaching aide. Three of the teachers are Anglo, three are Black, and the teaching aides are all Chicano or Black. Instruction in the learning center is carried out by a team which includes persons from all three racial groups. The follow through project, sponsored by Prentice-Hall Learning Systems, also includes inservice workshops for teachers and aides and regular consultant services.

PROCEDURES

The Metropolitan Achievement Test was administered to all children in October 1974 and again in May 1975. Also, a basic sight word test was administered tachistoscopically in the fall and again in the spring. Scores from 117 children who completed both pretests and posttests are used in this study.

Analysis of variance tests for the significance of differences among group scores were carried out by computer using the Statistical Package for the Social Sciences (SPSSH) version 6.00 program. Total Reading Standard Scores were used for comparisons on the Metropolitan Achievement Test. The number of words correctly identified from the list of 268 words were used for comparisons on the Basic Sight Word Vocabulary. Table 1 presents the number of children included in each class, grade, and racial group.

Table 1
Number of Children in Each Classroom, Grade, and Race Included in this Study

Grade	Classroom	Race			Total
		1	2	3	
1	1	5	6	3	14
	2	1	10	5	16
2	1	8	6	7	21
	2	3	8	9	20
3	1	2	5	15	22
	2	4	11	9	24
Total		23	46	48	117

An assumption of equality of performance at the beginning of the year is necessary for interpreting any comparison among racial groups on posttest scores. Means of the pretest Total Reading Standard Scores appear in Table 2. The assumption of equality was tested by analysis of variance. The results indicate no significant difference at any one grade level, but the seven point spread in standard scores cumulated over all three grade levels does represent a significant difference at the .05 level among the three racial groups in their reading performance at the beginning of the year. (A summary of the analysis appears in Table 3.) Therefore, in addition to a comparison of final test scores, a comparison of gain scores is also made. Gain scores were determined by simply subtracting each child's pretest score from his posttest score.

Table 2
Means of Pretest Total Reading Standard Scores from the Metropolitan Achievement Test

Grade	Classroom	Race 1	Race 2	Race 3	Total
1	1	27.2	27.8	28.33	27.71
	2	31.0	24.3	29.0	26.19
Total		27.83	25.63	28.75	26.9
2	1	41.38	40.83	36.71	39.6
	2	40.30	30.75	40.55	36.6
Total		41.09	35.07	38.80	38.17
3	1	46.5	47.4	50.50	49.45
	2	54.0	44.6	47.80	47.41
Total		51.5	45.5	49.54	48.39
Total		40.34	35.41	42.52	39.29

Table 3
Summary of Analysis of Variance Comparing Metropolitan Reading Pretest Standard Scores by Race for All Grades

Source	Sum of Squares	DF	Mean Square	F	P
Main Effects	8939.363	4	2234.841	40.02	.001*
Grade	7721.184	2	3860.592	69.133	.001*
Race	472.297	2	236.148	4.229	.017*
Interaction	46.031	4	11.508	.206	.99
Within	6031.024	108	55.843		
Total	15016.398	116	129.452		

*Significant

RESULTS OF THE ANALYSIS

Scores from three different sources were used to test the hypothesis that there is no difference in reading performance among the three racial groups: 1) Metropolitan Achievement Test, posttest Total Reading Standard Scores; 2) Gain scores derived from the difference between pretest and posttest standard scores; and 3) Basic Sight Word Test raw scores. The means of these scores for children in each class at each grade are presented in Tables 4, 5, and 6.

None of the comparisons by race, either at each grade level or across all grades, was found to be significant on any of the three measures. The difference in performance between the two first grade classrooms, apparent on all three measures, was found to be significant, but this difference appears to be constant across all three races.

Means over all grades on the posttest Total Reading Standard Scores are: Anglo, 50.04; Black, 46.06; and Chicano, 52.89. The mean gain scores over all grades are: Anglo, 9.69; Black, 10.65; and Chicano,

Table 4
Means of Posttest Total Reading Standard Scores
from the Metropolitan Achievement Test

Grade	Classroom	Race 1	Race 2	Race 3	Total
1	1	41.2	39.5	41.0	40.42
	2	38.0	32.7	35.8	34.0
Total		40.66	35.25	37.75	37.0
2	1	51.37	52.33	46.85	50.14
	2	42.66	45.87	53.22	48.7
Total		49.0	48.64	50.43	49.43
3	1	57.5	55.0	59.93	58.59
	2	63.25	54.45	59.0	57.62
Total		61.33	54.62	59.58	58.08
Total		50.04	46.06	52.89	49.64

Table 5
Means of Pretest to Posttest Gain Scores on
Metropolitan Total Reading Standard Scores

Grade	Classroom	Race 1	Race 2	Race 3	Total
1	1	14.000	11.667	12.667	12.714
	2	7.00	8.4	6.8	7.813
Total		12.833	5.136	6.188	10.10
2	1	10	11.5	10.143	10.476
	2	2.333	15.125	12.667	12.100
Total		7.909	13.571	11.563	11.268
3	1	11.00	7.6	9.4	9.136
	2	9.250	9.818	11.111	10.208
Total		9.833	9.125	10.042	9.696
Total		9.696	10.652	10.375	

Table 6
Means of Basic Sight Word Posttest Scores

Grade	Classroom	Race 1	Race 2	Race 3	Total
1	1	88	88.33	75.66	85.5
	2	78	23.5	48.2	34.62
Total		86.33	47.8	58.5	58.36
2	1	202.75	256.83	159.71	203.85
	2	184.33	161.75	241.33	200.95
Total		197.72	202.5	205.62	202.43
3	1	266.5	264.2	245.13	251.1
	2	263.5	246.81	263.44	255.83
Total		264.5	252.25	252.0	253.71
Total		180	173	171	174

Ratekin

10.37. Although the Black children scored somewhat lower on the posttest, they actually outperformed the other two groups in total gain over the year.

The analysis of variance summaries for comparing groups on the three measures across all grades appear in Tables 7, 8, and 9.

It should be pointed out that the children from the three groups not only made equal gain, but also that the progress they made represents a greater average growth than expected on the basis of previous performance by children at the same grade levels. In fact, the children in grade three made as much progress during the 1974-1975 year as they had made in their previous two years of instruction combined.

Table 7
Summary of Analysis of Variance Comparing Posttest
Metropolitan Total Reading Standard Scores
by Race for All Grades

Source	Sum of Squares	DF	Mean Square	F	P
Main Effects	8408.168	4	2102.042	25.45	.001*
Grade	7307.77	2	3653.889	44.24	.001*
Race	331.284	2	165.642	2.006	.137
Interaction	138.567	4	34.642	.419	.999
Within	8919.773	108	82.590		
Total	17466.508	116	150.573		

*Significant

Table 8
Summary of Analysis of Variance Comparing Metropolitan
Total Reading Gain Scores by Race for all Grades

Source	Sum of Squares	DF	Mean Square	F	P
Main Effects	79.089	4	19.772	.492	.999
Grade	65.011	2	32.506	.809	.999
Race	22.945	2	11.472	.286	.999
Interaction	243.139	4	60.785	1.513	.202
Within	4338.355	108	40.170		
Total	4660.586	116	40.177		

Table 9
Summary of Analysis of Variance Comparing Basic
Sight Word Scores by Race for All Grades

Source	Sum of Squares	DF	Mean Square	F	P
Main Effects	712972.437	4	178243.062	41.82	.001*
Grade	678525.750	2	339262.875	79.59	.001*
Race	2258.776	2	1129.388	.265	.999
Interaction	5426.187	44	1356.547	.318	.999
Within	460316.375	108	4262.187		
Total	1178715.00	116	10161.336		

*Significant

This progress is represented by a comparison of the percentile ranks achieved by the children at the beginning and at the end of the instructional period. The expected progress during the year would place the children on the same percentile rank as achieved at the beginning. Any increase in percentile rank represents a real advance over previous achievement. (This comparison is meaningless for grade one students since, theoretically, they would have received no previous direct instruction in reading as a basis for comparison.) The comparison for children in grades two and three appears in Table 10. The results indicate a dramatic change in performance—children in grade two progressed from the 24th to the 34th percentile, and children in grade three progressed from the 18th to the 40th percentile.

INTERPRETATION OF THE RESULTS

The results of this study support the conclusion that children from different linguistic backgrounds can profit equally from instruction in identical reading materials. Specialized materials, prepared to match dialect differences in phonology and grammar or prepared to represent specific cultural experiences, appear to be unnecessary for promoting significant progress in reading. This study was conducted in a setting where the teaching staff was aware of the concept of linguistic differences, and the teachers and aides were able to discriminate appropriate responses in relation to the oral language behavior of the children. The outcome agrees with the conclusions referred to above by Simons, and by Gibson and Levin, that a teacher's

Table 10
Percentile Ranks Achieved on Metropolitan Achievement Reading Tests at Pretest and Posttest by Children in Grades Two and Three

	Pretest		Posttest		
	Mean Standard Score	Percentile Rank	Mean Standard Score	Percentile Rank	Difference
Grade 2	38	24	49	34	+10
Grade 3	48	18	58	40	+22

knowledge of the factors of linguistic difference can make a real difference in the reading progress of linguistically different children without the use of specially prepared materials.

Evidently, the reading demands of materials related to children's levels of language development are of a different nature than demands related to language differences. Provision for language differences seem to be effectively made through the teaching relationship rather than through special content and language structures in instructional materials. Zintz (4) offers interesting examples of types of teacher interactions which may prove useful with linguistically different children.

It seems evident that basic linguistic concepts and firsthand experiences working with linguistically different children should comprise a significant segment of teacher education programs in reading.

References

1. Gibson, Eleanor, and Harry Levin. *The Psychology of Reading*. Cambridge, Massachusetts: MIT Press, 1975, 505-518.
2. Ruddell, Robet B. "Effect of Similarity of Oral and Written Patterns of Language Structure on Reading Comprehension," *Elementary English*, 42 (April 1965), 403-410.
3. Simons, Herbert D. "Black Dialect and Learning to Read," in Jerry L. Johns (Ed.), *Literacy for Diverse Learners*. Newark, Delaware: International Reading Association, 1974, 3-13.
4. Zintz, Miles V. *The Reading Process: The Teacher and the Learner*, Second Edition. Dubuque, Iowa: Wm. C. Brown, 1975, 397-457.

The Relationship between Sex Difference and Reading Ability in an Israeli Kibbutz System

Alice Dzen Gross
University of Rhode Island
Kingston, Rhode Island
United States of America

In this age of feminist inquiry, the quest for verification and explanation of presumed sex differences has taken on new force and dimension. Prior assumptions about sex-related characteristics are seriously being questioned and new evidence adduced to revise prevailing misconceptions.

It is with this spirit that four widely held assumptions about sex differences in reading were questioned. These assumptions were tested in a culture very different from the American culture.

The assumptions tested were that 1) girls in the elementary grades are better readers than boys; 2) girls are ready to read at an earlier age; 3) boys experience a higher incidence of reading disability and all other disabilities; and 4) (a derivation of 3) so universal a sex-linked phenomenon as male reading disability implies a physiological rather than cultural origin.

In general, the available evidence tends to lend credence to the first two assumptions. However, the data supporting such evidence derives primarily from American school systems. A different pattern emerges from the few available non-American studies. Here, results are dramatically opposed to American findings: specifically, two British studies *(3,9)* and one German study *(22)*.

The professional literature abounds with evidence substantiating the latter two assumptions, namely that a higher incidence of reading disability and other disabilities are found among boys and that the origin of male reading disability is physiological in nature. However, the clinical data serving as evidence are primarily American. The parochial limitation of these data raise doubts as to their universality. In addition, the reliability of the American data has come into question recently. Hobbs *(7)* attributes this unreliability to existent social and sexual biases of American culture. Despite the higher ratio in the direction of boys, reverse findings are reported from Germany *(22)* and Japan *(10)*.

Inconsistent and contradictory findings across cultures—with respect to sex differences in reading ability, reading disability, and reading readiness—raise doubts about the widely accepted physiological explanations for such differences.

The three physiological theories used most frequently by others to explain why more boys than girls are found among the reading disabled are: 1) *Maturational Lag*, boys' reading abilties are considered to lag behind girls' due to their slower rate of maturation; 2) *Crossed Dominance*, the lack of dominance of one cerebral hemisphere over the other is a condition purported to result in reading disability; and 3) *Vulnerability of the Male Organism*, the male organism's vulnerability to stress and trauma as well as its slower maturation accounts for male reading disabilities.

A closer scrutiny of the literature explicating the three physiological theories, lends further doubt as to their explanatory value in that internal contradictions also become apparent.

Such equivocal evidence warrants a reassessment of assumed sex differences in the area of reading. A need is warranted for data from cultures other than American.

This study was undertaken in order to overcome some of the inconsistencies found in these theories, as well as the equivocal evidence from other cultures.

The particular culture used to test these assumptions was a kibbutz system (a rural communal settlement) composed of 78 settlements within the state of Israel. Due to their philosophy and practices, this specific population is most appropriate to test hypotheses about sex differences. In particular, the lack of separation of boys and girls and the relative lack of differentiation of socialization practices helped clarify the roles physiology and socialization play in reading. The three physiological explanations, as put forth by western researchers, were tested with this population.

The first three research hypotheses advanced for this study were that no differences exist between kibbutz boys and kibbutz girls on the basis of 1) reading performance level, 2) reading readiness level, and 3) rate of maturational growth. The fourth and fifth research hypotheses advanced the ideas that no differences exist between kibbutz children on the basis of sex and reading level with respect to the correlates of 4) crossed dominance and 5) a psychopathology score.

Comparative data on boys and girls from a nonwestern culture should help clarify universal assumptions about sex differences in the areas of reading and disability. Among the unique attributes of the nonwestern culture selected for investigation were its clinical data. These data were available on all children within the society, hence allowing for a study of prevalence rates rather than the all too common incidence rates reported in American studies. In addition, these data were free of the social and sexual biases that contaminate American clinical data.

This study also addresses two other concerns regarding possible sex differences in reading. First, is the presumed greater prevalence of disabilities among boys. If the results confirm this supposition then, perhaps, boys should be liberated from our society's unrealistic expectations for them, and appropriate provision be made for their physiological differential.

On the other hand, if a greater prevalence of disability is not supported it will at least serve as a clue to an important finding about the role of cultural factors in the etiology of reading disabilities and other disabilities.

The kibbutz clinic was an ideal place in which to gather data on sex differences in numerous psychopathologies. It offered a rare opportunity for an accurate estimate of *prevalence* as compared to *incidence* of pathology.

One explanation for this advantageous position of the kibbutz clinic is the completeness and accuracy of health records from birth on. Through an investigation of the written records, the characteristics and problems of kibbutz children can be traced rather accurately from infancy to youth. Records included recorded observations of "metaplot" (caretakers) and teachers, as well as medical records. The high rate of population stability in the average kibbutz constitutes a supplementary asset.

A second advantage is the form of education. "Collective"education gives a more positive guarantee of early diagnosis than any other form of education. Since children grow up in a children's home, they are under observation by an objective eye from the first days of life. Metaplot, whose approach is more objective and less affective than that of parents, can be helpful to the latter in connection with overcoming their reluctance to consult professionals for advice. In a nonkibbutz family it is sometimes realized late that a child is handicapped (particularly a first child, because there is no other child against whom to compare development). Even when the parents sense that all is not well, they tend to overlook this, to delude themselves, because it is so difficult to face the truth and seek help.

A third advantage of kibbutz clinical data when attempting to determine prevalence rather than incidence of psychopathology, is the accessibility of the clinic to all members of the kibbutz population. There is no discrimination on the basis of financial resources, social status, or sex as exists in our society.

KIBBUTZ POPULATION

The kibbutz is a voluntary collective community. The main features are comprehensive communal living, communal ownership of property, and communal organization of production and consumption. Organized as a large household, the kibbutz contains a kitchen, a communal dining room, and several small dwelling units for both married and single members. Food, shelter, schooling, medical care, and entertainment are provided by the community. Politically, the community is governed as an ideal democracy by a general assembly of all members. Major decisions are determined jointly by a majority vote of the assembly membership.

In the early 1970s, there were some 200 kibbutzim in the country. The total population in these settlements is somewhat under 100,000 persons, less than 4 percent of the country's inhabitants. The vast majority of these kibbutzim are organized into three major federations that differ politically from left of center to extreme left. Kibbutz Artzi, the most leftist political federation as compared to the two other federations, has more consistently maintained its equality of the sexes principles in child rearing practices, as well as communal control of their education. From this federation (with a membership of 78 kibbutzim) was drawn the sample of kibbutz subjects of kindergarten, second, and fifth graders.

Table 1 lists the accessible population of kindergarten, second, and fifth graders in Kibbutz Artzi, in 1976.

Table 2 lists the numbers within that population that served as the subjects for the sample within this study.

Table 1
Grade and Sex Distribution of Kibbutz Artzi Population*

Grade	Boys	Girls	Marginal Total
K	316	297	613
Second	284	256	540
Fifth	350	368	718
Marginal Totals	950	921	1871 = Total Population

*Statistics gathered from Oranim Research Institute of Kibbutz Education, Kiryat Tivon, Haifa.

Table 2
Grade and Sex Distribution of Tested Sample
of Kibbutz Artzi Population*

Grade	Boys	Girls	Marginal Total
K	42	55	97
Second	53	46	99
Fifth	54	55	109
Marginal Totals	149	156	305 = Total Sample Population

*Total grade population tested within the following eight kibbutzim:
Bet-Alpha, Mishmar-Ha-Emek, Sarid, Merchavia, Shar-Hamakim, Gazit, Ein-Dor.

INSTRUMENTATION

Ortar's Hebrew Reading Comprehension Test (20) served as a reading performance measure. Ninety-nine second graders and 108 fifth graders were administered this test during January and February of 1976. The scores on the reading test served as a basis for testing the first hypothesis, and answering the question, "Are sex differences in reading as evident on the Israeli kibbutzim as in other societies?" These scores were further used to discriminate two subgroups within the tested population; superior readers and disabled readers. Subgroup scores were further analyzed for sex differences and percentages of reading disability cases. The criterion for a superior reader was a score within the 99-100 percentile of the Israeli norms. The criterion for a disabled reader was a score within the lowest 15 percent of the individual's class as well as his/her referral for reading remediation. In March 1976, the two subgroups, differentiated by reading level, were revisited. On this visit, they were administered the V-Tube Eyedness Test and the Edinburgh Handedness Inventory Test (2) for crossed dominance. The findings served as a basis for testing the Crossed Dominance hypothesis.

In addition, these two subgroups were evaluated on twelve additional indices of psychopathology: 1) organic speech defects, 2) cerebral palsy, 3) epilepsy, 4) mental retardation, 5) schizophrenia, 6) minimal brain damage, 7) premature birth, 8) pregnancy complications, 9) birth complications, 10) emotional disturbance, 11) sight defects, and 12) hearing defects.

These data were derived from careful examination of the medical records of those children seen at the central kibbutz clinic. The nature of this distinction permitted an adequate test of Bentzen's hypothesis (1) that psychopathologic conditions, including reading disability, are three to ten times more frequent among elementary school boys than girls of the same grade level.

The Bender-Gestalt Visual Motor Coordination Test served as both a reading readiness and a maturational measure. Forty-two kindergarten boys and fifty-five kindergarten girls were administered this test in a ten minute session during a four week period in January 1976. Their scores were used as the data with which to test the Maturational Lag hypothesis. Koppitz's Rating System (14) was employed on all test protocols.

PRESENTATION OF RESULTS

The following presentation will include a statement of each operational hypothesis and its accompanying data analysis, followed by statements of acceptance or rejection of the hypothesis.

Hypothesis 1.1: Kibbutz boys and girls in grades two and five will show no significant differences in reading performance as evidenced by a comparison of the mean male reading test score to the mean female reading test score. A *t* test was performed on the scores for each grade with results summarized in Tables 3 and 4.

Hypothesis 1.1 is accepted as stated. No significant difference was found between the mean score for boys and the one for girls. In fact, the integer mean scores for both sexes in the second grade were exactly the same ($\bar{x} = 40$), and the integer mean scores for both sexes in the fifth grade differed by only two points: Boys, $\bar{x} = 41$ and Girls, $\bar{x} = 39$.

Hypothesis 1.2: The percentage of male reading disabled within a sample of kibbutz children in second and fifth grades will not disclose a different percentage than that of the female reading disabled.

A nonstatistical analysis was undertaken in order to compute the percentages needed to test this hypothesis. The results are summarized in Table 5.

Table 3
t Test for Differences between Means in Reading Scores, by Sex, in Second Grade Kibbutz Children

Sex	n	$\bar{X}$	S.D.	S.E.	t	df
Boys	50	40.18	10.73	1.51	0.28 n.s.	94
Girls	49	40.76	9.29	1.37		

Table 4
t Test for Differences between Means in Reading Scores, by Sex, in Fifth Grade Kibbutz Children

Sex	n	$\bar{X}$	S.D.	S.E.	t	df
Boys	52	40.63	9.43	1.30	1.18 n.s.	100
Girls	50	38.66	7.32	1.03		

Table 5
Percentages of Reading Disability, by Sex,
within Kibbutz Second and Fifth Grades

Sex	n	Reading Disabled	Percent of Population
Boys	102	13	12.50
Girls	96	12	12.75

Thirteen percent of the boys and 13 percent of the girls were found to be reading disabled. Therefore, hypothesis 1.2 was accepted as stated. Due to the self-evident similarity in percentages obtained, it was not deemed necessary to pursue these proportions with a statistical test. The preceding findings are the reverse of the findings in other countries. A summary of the United States studies dealing with sex ratio in reading disabilities is presented in Table 6 to point up this strong contrast.

Table 6
Summary of Sex Ratios in Reading Disability
at Elementary School Age*

Study in Chronological Order	Boys	Ratio :	Girls
Monroe (1932)	8	:	1
Kopel & Geerded (1933)	8	:	1
Olson (1940)	4-9	:	1
Durrell (1956)	10	:	1
Kanner (1957)	15	:	1
Bentzen (1963)	3	:	1
Critchley (1964)	5	:	1
Wyatt (1966)	9	:	1
Isom (1957)	6	:	1
Mumpower (1970)	3	:	1
Harris, A.J. (1970)	8	:	1
Rice (1970)	5	:	1
Maccoby & Jacklin (1974	3-10	:	1

*Studies are cited in references at end of chapter.

Hypothesis 2: Kibbutz boys in kindergarten will show no significant difference, between means, with kibbutz girls in kindergarten on a reading readiness (Bender-Gestalt) test.

Hypothesis 3: Kibbutz boys in kindergarten will show no significant difference, between means, with kibbutz girls in kindergarten on a test for rate of maturational development (Bender-Gestalt).

The Bender-Gestalt served as a dual measure in this investigation. The literature supports its use as both a reading readiness measure and as a maturational measure. Therefore, the results are summarized simultaneously for hypothesis 2 and hypothesis 3 in Table 7.

Hypotheses 2 and 3 were accepted as stated. No significant difference was demonstrated by sex, on the mean scores for the Bender-Gestalt test.

Each of the three physiological theories noted earlier, purporting to explain a higher incidence of reading disability among boys, was subjected to empirical testing.

Maturational Lag was the first physiological theory that was tested by hypothesis 3. In brief, it theorizes that girls are considered to be more advanced developmentally than boys and, thus, are ready to read sooner. Hypothesis 3 was accepted as stated.

The second physiological theory to be tested was that of crossed dominance. In capsule form, this theory suggests that reading disability results from lack of dominance of one cerebral hemisphere. The condition of incomplete or crossed dominance is reported to be more prevalent among boys than girls. It is on this basis that reading problems are said to occur more frequently among boys than girls.

Table 7
t Test for Differences between Means of Bender
Scores, by Sex, for Kibbutz Children,
Ages Six to Six and One-Half

Sex	n	$\overline{X}$	S.D.	t
Boys	42	7.02	5.24	
Girls	55	6.45	5.62	.5 n.s.

Hypothesis 4.1: Kibbutz boys in grades two and five who are classified as reading disabled will not show a significant difference on a test for crossed dominance as compared with Kibbutz girls in grades two and five classified as reading disabled.

Hypothesis 4.2: Kibbutz boys and girls in grades two and five, who are classified as reading disabled, will not show a significant difference on a test for crossed dominance as compared to a matched kibbutz group who are classified as superior readers.

Hypothesis 4.3: Kibbutz boys in grades two and five, who are classified as reading disabled, will not show a significant difference on a test for crossed dominance as compared to kibbutz boys in grades two and five classified as superior readers.

A two-way chi-square analysis of the data was performed for each of the preceding hypotheses dealing with crossed dominance. The results are illustrated in chi-square tables 8, 9 and 10.

Table 8
Two-Way Chi-Square Analysis of Sex by
Cerebral Dominance

	Cerebral Dominance	Crossed Dominance	Total
Reading Disabled Boys	7	6	13
	53.8	46.2	52.0
	53.8	50.0	52.0
	28.0	24.0	
Reading Disabled Girls	6	6	12
	50.0	50.0	48.0
	46.2	50.0	
	24.0	24.0	
Column Total	13	12	25
	52.0	48.0	100.0

Corrected Chi-Square = 0.04 with 1 degree of freedom n.s.

Table 9
Two-Way Chi-Square Analysis of Reading Level by Cerebral Dominance

	Cerebral Dominance	Crossed Dominance	Total
Reading Disabled	13	12	25
	52.0	48.0	26.9
	26.0	27.9	
	14.0	12.9	
Superior Readers	37	31	68
	54.4	45.6	73.1
	74.0	72.1	
	39.8	33.3	
Column Total	50	43	93
	53.8	46.2	100.0

Corrected Chi-Square = 0.00 with a 1 degree of freedom n.s.

Table 10
Two-Way Chi-Square Analysis of Male Reading Level by Cerebral Dominance

	Cerebral Dominance	Crossed Dominance	Total
Disabled Boy Readers	7	6	13
	53.8	46.2	23.6
	21.2	27.3	
	12.7	10.9	
Superior Boy Readers	26	16	42
	61.9	38.1	76.4
	78.8	72.7	
	47.3	29.1	
Column Total	33	22	55
	60.0	40.0	100.0

Corrected Chi-Square = 0.04 with 1 degree of freedom n.s.

All hypotheses were confirmed as stated. In other words, on the variable of crossed dominance, no significant differences had been shown to exist between reading disabled boys and reading disabled girls; between a reading disabled population and a superior reading population; and between reading disabled boy readers and superior boy readers.

The third, and last, physiological theory to be tested was the Vulnerability of the Male Organism theory. This theory describes the male organism as much more vulnerable to stress and trauma than the female organism. It is this vulnerability which is purported to account for the higher male incidence in reading disability. This theory was tested in the form of the following two hypotheses.

Hypothesis 5.1: An analysis of the medical records of kibbutz boys and girls in grades two and five, defined as reading disabled, will not disclose a statistically significant difference in a psychopathology score between sexes.

Hypothesis 5.2: An analysis of the medical records of kibbutz girls and boys defined as superior readers will not disclose a statistically significant difference in a psychopathology score between sexes.

The same thirteen psychopathological indicators employed by Bentzen *(1)* in support of her theory were employed in this study. Results are shown in tables 11 and 12.

Hypothesis 5.1 is accepted as stated. A difference was found (.03) though not significant at the accepted (.01) level of significance. Furthermore, the difference was found in a direction contrary to the predicted direction of the theory tested. It was the *girls* rather than the *boys* who demonstrated the higher psychopathology score. Such significance can probably be explained as a negative by-product when a test is employed on the same population more than twice.

Hypothesis 5.2 is accepted as stated. No significant difference (0.11) was found between superior male readers and superior female readers on the means of a psychopathology score.

DISCUSSION OF RESULTS

One general aim of this study was to test several assumptions about girls being better readers. Related to this was the test of several theories purporting to explain this seemingly sex-linked phenomenon.

Table 11
t Test for Differences between Mean Scores, by Sex,
on a 13 Point Psychopathology Index for Kibbutz
Reading Disabled Children

Variable	n	X̄	S.D.	S.E.	t	df
Reading Disabled Boys	14	1.35	1.33	0.35		
Reading Disabled Girls	12	2.66	1.55	0.44	-2.31 n.s.	24

Table 12
t Test for Differences between Means Scores, by Sex,
on a 13 Point Psychopathology Index for Kibbutz
Superior Reading Children

Variable	n	X̄	S.D.	S.E.	t	df
Superior Boy Readers	43	0.67	0.74	0.11		
Superior Girl Readers	26	0.96	0.66	0.13	-1.61 n.s.	67

Results of analyses of reading performance level and reading readiness level among Israeli kibbutz children indicated no significant sex differences. However, the study disclosed that the Israelis have not yet developed a standardized means for identifying reading readiness. Despite the impressive results obtained with the instrument employed, namely that no sex differences were observed in reading readiness, the limitations of the instrument make such observations questionable. The question of sex differences in reading readiness must await reexamination by a more reliable instrument. At the time of this study, no standardized measure for reading readiness was available in Israel. However, two good instruments were in the process of being translated and standardized. One is the Wepman-Roswell Test by Irma T. Auerbach (Yeshiva University), and the other is Katrina de Hirsch's *Predictive Index* by Daryn (Oranim Clinic). No gender differences were evident in percentage of reading disability cases and in level of maturational development. Crossed dominance, and twelve additional indices of psychopathology were found to be unrelated to cases of male reading disability. Therefore, these analyses do not lend support to the physiological theories in this study purporting to explain male reading disability.

IMPLICATIONS

This investigation into the kibbutz culture disclosed an equally high level of reading performance for both sexes. In part, this may be attributed to cultural influences. Such evidence should contribute to a rethinking of prevailing attitudes and practices in societies where boys demonstrate difficulties in reading.

It should give educators pause to reconsider current popular American recommendations such as delayed school entrance for boys and sex-grouped reading instruction. Among the proponents for such recommendations are Stauffer *(25)*, Pauley *(21)*, Wilson *(26)*, Kern-Kamp and Price *(12)*, Lyles *(15)*, and Scheiner *(24)*.

The underlying purposes for such approaches are to alleviate the lowered self-esteem experienced by boys. Paradoxically, however, the converse tends to be true. One would suspect that these practices crystallize what, initially, may have been fairly pliant cultural distinctions between the sexes, thereby contributing additional impetus to a pervasive sterotyping. Such sterotyping, regardless of its origin or intent, can only delimit individual freedom.

The focus on cultural variables in this study does not imply any denial of those fairly well-established medical findings which show that certain pathologies are sex-linked organically. Rather, the rationale for such a focus was to present evidence which is supportive of the often dismissed component of culture for diagnoses and treatment of such pathologies.

In American clinics we do not have data on the number of children who may actually experience reading disability but, rather, for those subjects with whom someone saw fit to take some sort of action, thereby making these cases accessible to researchers.

The true prevalence of reading disability is not yet known. This kibbutz study based on a total population is more likely to approximate it than a survey of clinics and remedial reading classes in the United States and other western countries. This study was limited to determining whether boys in kibbutz read as well as girls, and whether they suffer a higher frequency of disabilities than girls. In all instances, kibbutz boys and girls were found to be similar. This finding stands out in contrast to western findings.

Hopefully, these data can serve as a foundation upon which subsequent research can build a clearer understanding of those aspects of kibbutz upbringing which promote similarly high performance from each sex. In pursuit of such understanding, it is recommended that the following speculations of kibbutz structure be explored.

1. *Coeducation.* A socialization system by which both sexes share sleeping and living quarters and are expected to relate together as equals. They also attend school together from infancy through adolesence. The implication of this form of childrearing should be studied in detail to clarify its role in promoting school-related activities as sex-appropriate for both boys and girls and, more significantly, what implications lie therein as antecedents for equally high levels of achievement.

2. *Progressive schooling.* A permissive educational system where grading and testing are rejected and special tutoring is accepted as the "norm." This form of schooling might be making the appropriate individualized educational provisions for each sex, thereby avoiding the problems encountered in American education.

3. *Comprehensive health services.* Services are offered both as preventive and therapeutic. In addition, they are accessible to all kibbutz children. Perhaps so comprehensive a service protects the more vulnerable male organism from realizing its vulnerability to many pathologies?

These speculations and many others leave much to be explored. This study was only limited to ascertaining whether boys in kibbutz read as well as girls and whether they suffer a higher frequency of disabilities than girls. The cultural origin of these findings still eludes precise scientific explanations. It is hoped that those questions raised by this study will serve to stimulate an expanded search for cultural origins of reading and learning problems.

References

1. Bentzen, Frances. "Sex Ratios in Learning and Behavior Disorders," *American Journal of Orthopsychiatry,* 33 (1963), 92-98.
2. Bond, Guy, and Miles Tinker. *Reading Difficulties: Their Diagnosis and Correction.* New York: Appleton-Century-Crofts, 1973.
3. Brimer, M. A. "Sex Differences in Listening Comprehension," *Journal of Research and Development in Education,* 3 (1969), 72-79.
4. Critchley, MacDonald. *Developmental Dyslexia.* London: Heinemann, 1964.
5. Durrell, Donald. *Improving Reading Instruction.* New York: Harcourt Brace Jovanovich, 1956.
6. Harris, Albert J. *How to Increase Reading Ability.* New York: David McKay, 1970.
7. Hobbs, Nichols. *The Futures of Children: Categories, Labels, and Their Consequences.* San Francisco: Josscy Bass, 1975.
8. Isom, John B. "Some Neuropsychological Findings in Children with Reading Problems," in Malcolm P. Douglass (Ed.), *Self and Society,* Claremont, California: Claremont Reading Conference, 1967.
9. Johnson, Dale D. "Sex Differences in Reading Across Cultures," *Reading Research Quarterly,* 9 (1973-1974), 67-86.
10. Kagan, Jerome. "Sex Typing During the Preschool and Early School Years," in Irving Janis, et al. (Eds.), *Personality: Dynamics, Development, and Assessment.* New York: Harcourt Brace Jovanovich, 1969, 490.
11. Kanner, L. *Child Psychiatry* (3rd ed.). Springfield, Illinois: Charles C. Thomas, 1957.
12. KernKamp, Emily, and Eleanor Price. "Coeducation May Be a 'No-No' for the Six-Year-Old Boy," *Phi Delta Kappan,* 53 (June 1972), 662-663.
13. Kopel, David, and H. Geerded. "A Survey of Clinical Services for Poor Readers," *Journal of Educational Psychology,* 13 (1933), 209-224.
14. Koppitz, Elizabeth M. *The Bender Gestalt Test for Young Children: Volume II.* New York: Grune and Stratton, 1975.
15. Lyles, Thomas B. "Grouping by Sex," *National Elementary School Principal,* 46 (November 1966), 384-441.
16. Maccoby, Eleanor E., and Carol N. Jacklin. *The Psychology of Sex Differences.* Stanford, California: Stanford University Press, 1974.
17. Monroe, Marion. *Children Who Cannot Read.* Chicago: Chicago University Press, 1932.
18. Mumpower, D. L. "Sex Ratios Found in Various Types of Referred Exceptional Children," *Exceptional Children,* 23 (April 1970), 621-626.
19. Olson, W. C. *Child Development.* New York: D. C. Heath, 1940.

20. Ortar, Gina. *Reading Tests for Elementary School Grades*. Jerusalem: Ministry of Education, 1975.
21. Pauley, Frank R. "Sex Differences and Legal School Entrance Age," *Journal of Educational Research*, 1 (September 1951), 1-9.
22. Preston, Ralph C. "Reading Achievement of German and American Children," *School and Society*, 90 (October 1962), 350-354.
23. Rice, Donald B. "Learning Disabilities: An Investigation in Two Parts," *Journal of Learning Disabilities*, 3 (1970), 149-155.
24. Scheiner, Louis. "A Pilot Study to Assess the Academic Progress of Disadvantaged First Graders Assigned to Class by Sex and Taught by a Teacher of the Same Sex," School District of Philadelphia, November 1969. Eric, Ed. No. 035462.
25. Stauffer, Russell. "Do Sex Differences Affect Reading?" *The Instructor*, May 1968, 25.
26. Wilson, Elizabeth. "Sex Differences in the Elementary School: A Discussion," *National Elementary School Principal*, 46 (November 1966), 8-12.
27. Wyatt, Nita M. "The Reading Achievement of First Grade Boys Vs. First Grade Girls," *Reading Teacher*, 19 (May 1966), 661-665.

The Relationship of Syntax to Readability for ESL Students in Thailand

Sirirat Nilagupta
Kasetsart University
Bangkok, Thailand

For many years researchers have been investigating factors that affect the readability of prose. Some have found that vocabulary and sentence length affected readability, and these two variables were taken into account in developing readability formulas.

Others believed that in order to understand the meaning of sentences, readers need to know much more than the meaning of the individual words of which they are constructed *(30)*. They must be able to understand the language structures through which ideas, information, and concepts are conveyed.

The rules of syntax are not just the rules that the writer applies to organize his statements—they are the rules he assumes the receiver knows in order to be able to extract the meaning from statements. For the reader, grammar and syntax are the keys to comprehending the language.

The present article reports on an investigation of the effect of syntax on the comprehension of written English by Thai college students who have studied English as a foreign language. The research pinpointed specific structures which are likely to cause difficulty for nonnative speakers. Interestingly, a review of the literature shows they are the same structures which perplex native speakers.

Reprinted from *Journal of Reading*, 20 (April 1977), 585-594.

EARLIER STUDIES ON SYNTAX

The relationship between reading ability and knowledge of grammar has been investigated for several decades. Over forty years ago Ojemann *(28)* analyzed adult reading materials, looking for those factors which would prove difficult for adults with less than an eighth grade education. He suggested simplified sentence structure—especially, fewer prepositions. Later, Gibbons *(14)* explored the relationship between recognizing sentence parts and comprehending the whole sentence meaning, finding that this was an essential skill for reading.

In 1956, Strom *(32)* found a correlation between the ability to read materials of an informative or literary nature and the ability to analyze the syntax and grammar of the sentences read. It was .57 for public school students and .39 for private school students.

O'Donnell *(26)*, working with high school seniors, concluded there was no conclusive evidence that the teaching of linguistic structures would assist in developing reading comprehension, although the results did not prove that an ability to recognize structural relationships was not important in reading comprehension.

DeLancey *(9)* used nonsense words to determine a student's ability to recognize linguistic relationships. The result showed that the ability to recognize form classes was a factor (although not a major one) in both fifth and, to a lesser extent, ninth grade students' reading comprehension.

Hunt *(20)* noted that the clause length of passages increased steadily from grade four through nine, both in adult produced reading materials and in student writing samples. He concluded that increased difficulty in reading sentences usually results from increased clause length.

After Chomsky *(2)* presented his theory (now known as transformational grammar), researchers began to apply it to readability factors. Transformational grammar proposes that all English sentences are composed of one or more simple sentences, called "kernel sentences." The kernel sentences can be variously rephrased in what is called "transformations." The rephrasings may be spliced into other sentences at appropriate points, a process known as "embedding."

The kernel sentence consists of the simplest subject, verb, and predicate structure allowable in English. In this form, it is the epitome of redundant expressive units. It helps listeners and readers to predict its major words.

As each new transformed sentence is embedded into the kernel or conjoined onto it, the expanded kernel becomes less and less of an aid to predicting its major words. In fact, each embedded or conjoined transformation not only disrupts the redundancy within itself, but since transformation often rearranges normal word order, it also results in the deletion of inflectional endings *(11)*.

Among the more active researchers in this field is Coleman *(5)*, who found that college readers increased their comprehension slightly when all subordinate clauses were rewritten as independent sentences. Later, Coleman and Blumenfeld *(7)* found that reading comprehension increased significantly when nominalizations were rewritten as sentences with appropriate subjects inserted. One year later, Coleman *(4)* conducted a study in which he detransformed four difficult sentence structures: nominalizations, passive-voice constructions, relative clauses, and deletions. The readers who read the simplified detransformed materials scored significantly better on cloze tests.

Mehler *(23)* tested the ability to recall kernel sentences that were transformed in four ways: passives, questions, negatives, and combinations of the three. Simple, direct kernel statements, both negative and passive, were recalled best, followed in increasing difficulty by single-transformation questions, double-transformations, and passive plus negative. Clark *(3)* also found that recall was inhibited by the passive voice construction.

Fagan *(12)* found that embedding (the inserting of one kernel into another) and deletion (the leaving out of unnecessarily redundant words) correlated more highly with reading difficulty than did other transformations. The following structures were most difficult: appositive; *ing*-nominalization; pronoun (genitive); common elements deletions; and negative. However, contrary to Fodor and Garrett's *(13)* findings, it was not the number of transformations within a sentence but, rather, their complexity which correlated with difficulty.

Nurss *(24)* discovered that sentences with fewer embeddings (or relative clause insertions) were significantly easier for students to comprehend in both oral and silent reading.

CONTRIBUTING FACTORS

It may be concluded from the research findings that the following five syntactic factors have contributed to readability difficulty: negatives, passive voice construction, embedding, deletion, and nominalization.

If those syntax factors affect readability for those whose native language is English, then to what extent do they affect nonnative speakers of English such as Japanese, Chinese, or Thai? Goodman and Fleming *(16)* suggested that the native speaker approaches reading like a "psycholinguistic guessing game." This process involves: 1) sampling graphic, syntactic, and semantic cues; 2) predicting both structure and meaning on the basis of these selected cues; 3) testing the prediction; and 4) either confirming that prediction or correcting if necessary.

When a native speaker reads, he or she scans a line and fixes at a point to permit the eyes to focus. He or she picks up graphic cues and makes a guess — a prediction about what appears on the printed page. While this guess is partly based on graphic cues, it also results from the reader's knowledge about the language and what he has read up to that point. If his guess makes semantic and syntactic sense, he continues to read. If it doesn't, a recheck is made and the guess is amended.

Native speakers of English have receptive control over virtually all of the English syntax and productive control over most of it. They have acquired an extensive vocabulary. Thus, they learned to read more or less well to the extent that they perceived the relationship of written English and spoken English.

Those who study English as a foreign language obviously cannot be expected to make such predictions rapidly. They may be unable to recognize the uninformative features because to them all features should be informative.

In Thai, the writing system is different from that of English. The syntax is also quite different. English inflections, word order, and function words are different from those of Thai. Yet the reader depends upon these factors to transmit meaning. Thais learning to read may expect that the word order in English will in some way resemble the word order in Thai; for example, in the Thai language adjectives follow the nouns they modify and frequently are taken for verbs in sentences. The reader must perceive that the word order is more important than are inflections in English — that it carries more information. The reader must control a great deal of grammar in order to select only the most significant cues.

Semantic cues offer further confusion. The student may recognize the word in one context but not in another. He or she may comprehend the literal meaning without recognizing the author's real point.

Sampling graphic, syntactic, and semantic cues may be quite an obstacle for the nonnative speaker of English who may not know which units store the most information.

THAI GRADUATE STUDENTS

The writer conducted a pilot study to determine if there was a significant relationship between Thai students' ability to interpret syntactic structure and their ability to comprehend English written materials. For this, student scores on tests of structure comprehension and reading comprehension were compared.

These subjects were graduates from several universities in Thailand who had applied for admission to the National Institute of Development Administration. This is a graduate school with four colleges — Public Administration, Business Administration, Applied Statistics, and Development Economics.

The English Screening Test was administered to 1278 students. The three-hour test consisted of three subtests—Vocabulary, Structure Comprehension (twenty-five sentences with various types of structure), and Reading Comprehension (four passages with thirty multiple choice questions).

For this study, only the scores from the Structure Comprehension Subtest and from the Reading Comprehension Subtest were analyzed. The data were selected by taking every third answer sheet from the whole of 1278. There were 426 altogether.

Correlation coefficients (Pearson Product-Moment) were done using each subject's scores on the two subtests. The obtained correlation coefficient was .54 [t (424) = 13.2, $p < .001$]. Thus, there was a positive relationship between student scores on structure comprehension and on reading comprehension.

SOURCES OF DIFFICULTY

Analysis of student performance on individual test items revealed an accordance with earlier research studies that had used native speakers of English: the syntactic factors contributing to readability difficulty for Thai students, too. Those factors are:

1. *Negative words.* The Structure Comprehension Subtest revealed that the most difficult sentence was: "By no means do I suggest that individuals have direct freedom to act on their own." The percentage correct for this item was only 16.

What might cause difficulty in reading this sentence are the embedded noun clause, the infinitive phrase, the pronoun genitive, and irregular word order (inversion of subject and verb). But after examining carefully the four choices, the writer discovered that the students had greatest difficulty with the expression "by no means."

In addition, it was noticed that other items that contained such negative words as "not," "no," "none," "neither . . . nor" were evidently difficult to process.

2. *Passive voice* verb construction. Naturally, Thai students found passive voice verb constructions difficult to process, for they are seldom used in either speech or writing of the Thai language. When they are used, only one prefix is placed before the verb. Furthermore, Thai verbs never have inflectional endings.

Among the test items the students found difficult were: a) "The government's police power can be used in other ways to provide necessary labor." and b) "Mass media have been accused of making people think and behave alike but on some people the mass media have the opposite effect."

Thirty-three percent of the students passed item (a), 50 percent item (b). Thus the students found sentence (b) easier in spite of its length. This is in agreement with the findings of Glazer *(15)* who viewed long sentences resulting from the connection of simple kernel sentences as easy to process. Sentence (b) was the result of the three simple kernel sentences joined by "and" and "but."

Although there were other syntactic factors such as deletion and gerundial phrase, the investigation of the four choices of this test item confirmed that the passive voice verb construction caused serious reading difficulties.

Sentence (a), which was not so long as sentence (b), proved to be more difficult. It also contained a passive voice verb construction, but since there were a genitive noun and a noun adjunct, it was quite difficult to determine which element caused the difficulty.

3. *Embedding.* Undoubtedly, embedding does contribute to reading difficulty for Thai students. Almost all of the test items of the Structure Comprehension Subtest contained one or more embedded sentences.

Here is an example: a) "Since World War II a new strain of rubber tree has been developed which yields several times as much latex as the pre-war did." The percentage correct for this item was 23.

An embedded relative clause found in this sentence was the most difficult because the antecedent of the relative pronoun "which" was not a noun or pronoun but the whole sentence that came before it. Moreover, there was a comparison clause embedded in the relative clause, and both passive voice verb construction and deletion were included.

Another example: b) "A 78-year-old woman went to prison for three months yesterday rather than pay a 19.08 sterling tax bill which she said had been assessed on wrongful principles."

Even if we exclude a modifier before a noun ("78-year-old woman") as a transformation of an embedded sentence, three other embedded sentences were found in this sentence — a relative clause in the comparison clause, and a noun clause in the relative clause. The percentage correct for this was 32.

4. *Deletion.* Deletion was found as difficult to process as embedding. In the above examples, both 3a and 3b contained deletion factors. The students would find sentence 3a much easier if it were rewritten as ". . . which yields several times as much latex as the pre-war [tree] did."

The deletion of the subject of the verb "pay" in sentence 3b was not so difficult since "woman" was the only subject in this sentence who could "pay."

The following sentence proved to be very difficult: "The county agent has much less research training, but still enough to know what help or information to ask for." Due to the deletion, 66 percent of the students failed this item. They were not aware that this sentence could be rewritten as "The county agent has much less research training, but *the country agent* still has enough *research training* to know what help or information to ask for."

5. *Nominalization.* The nominalization specified in previous research studies as a factor of reading difficulty was the derivational nominalization (for example, the *production* of good) and the gerundive nominalization (the *improving* of health). Only one item in this subtest contained derivational nominalization: "In a number of the countries a start is being made on the introduction of educational and manpower aspects into development planning."

Since there were a lot of factors that may contribute to the difficult comprehension of this sentence (such as passive voice verb construction, modifier load, and nominalization) and since Thai students are quite used to derivational nominalization in their native language, this writer hesitated to make a conclusion that the nominalization factor affected readability of English texts for Thai students.

OTHER FACTORS

Besides the five factors mentioned, what should be taken into consideration were modifier load, pronoun substitution, and modals. When Granowsky developed his Syntactic Complexity Formula in 1972, he assigned weights to modifiers and modals besides other elements of the language.

Although a single modifier before a noun may not cause much reading difficulty to native speakers of English, Thai students (among others) may find it difficult to understand because in their native language nouns precede their modifiers.

The students would find noun adjuncts even more difficult to process. In such a sentence as "The brick house is blown away by the hurricane," the students may have a problem with the head noun. They could not decide which was blown away, the "brick" or "house." The more noun modifiers there are, the more confused the students become.

In the sentence that has already been mentioned, "In a number of countries a start is being made on the introduction of educational and manpower aspects into development planning." the students who recognized the inflectional ending would have no problem with the word "educational" but when they came across "manpower" they might wonder whether "a start is being made on the introduction of manpower" or "a start is being made on the introduction of aspects." Moreover, "development" is a noun and "planning" looks like a verb. Naive students would have difficulty in detecting which was the head noun, "development" or "planning."

A verb used as a predicative adjective can be mistaken as a main verb. One item of the test contained the sentence, "The incident was embarrassing to me, and it could have been avoided." The percentage correct for this item was only 26.

Two factors that might have caused difficulty were the participle "embarrassing" used as a modifier of the noun "incident," and the verb phrase "could have been avoided."

According to the sentence structure, the students may interpret the content in two ways:

The incident	*was embarrassing*	*to me*
subject	verb	

The incident	*was embarrassing*		*to me*
subject	verb	modifier	

As for the modal, two test items that contained modals proved to be difficult for Thai students. They were: a) "The incident was embarrassing to me, and it could have been avoided." and b) "If those men had realized he was president of his company, they might not have talked so freely." The percentage correct for sentence (a) was 26, and for sentence (b), 41.

Previous research studies revealed that a sentence containing a clause was more difficult to process than two or more simple kernel sentences joined by "and," "but," or other frequently used conjunctions. Contrary to this, sentence (a) proved to be more difficult.

Both of these items contained modals—the first sentence a passive voice verb construction modal and the second sentence a negative construction modal. What made sentence (a) more difficult may be both the position of the modifier "embarrassing" and the difficulty in interpreting the string of verbs "could have been avoided." Many students do not recognize the contrary-to-fact meaning of such strings of verbs.

The second sentence contained a conditional clause. Again, when they encountered "might not have talked," the students could not relate this surface structure to its semantic representation. They did not know that this sentence could be rewritten as "Those men did not realize he was president of his company and so they talked quite freely."

Look at these other two sentences: a) "Ann should sweep the floor." and b) "Ann should have been sweeping the floor." Sentence (b) is clearly more difficult, but according to Granowsky's formula all modals are given one count each.

Such modals as "will," "can," and "do" are not difficult because of the frequency of their use. The grammar of modal verbs is not complex, but the semantics is. Modals refer to the probability of occurrence or imply a moral judgment about occurrence; there may even be a slight ambiguity about which is meant.

Though simple grammatically, the abstractness of their meaning and the possible ambiguity of their interpretation make modal verbs difficult to process (8).

UNSUSPECTED DIFFICULTIES

The different levels of difficulty of the same type of structure have led this writer to question the accuracy of the weight given to each aspect of syntax. The weight seems to be assigned on the basis of the type of structure, such as modal, phrases, or clauses. The discussion of the modal above was a clear example of structures of the same type which were nevertheless different in respect to difficulty of processing.

Other examples were a relative clause and an appositive phrase. In this writer's opinion, not all embedded relative clauses and appositive phrases cause difficulty in comprehension. In terms of syntax they may, but frequently the writers use a clause or phrase modifier to provide clues to the intended meaning of a word. Here is an example: "A tourniquet, which is a device for stopping bleeding by twisting something tightly against an artery, has already been applied to the wound."

Instead of causing difficulty, the relative clause above facilitates comprehension. It provides a helpful definition of the word "tourniquet."

This is quite the same for an appositive phrase since it is the relative clause with the deletion of the relative pronoun and the copula.

If an appositive provides clues to the meaning of hard words, the appositive cannot be considered a factor inhibiting comprehension.

Frequently, it is the semantic and not the syntactic factor that causes different types of adverbials to vary in difficulty. Though structurally more complex than one-word adverbs, a great many prepositions frequently used to introduce phrases meaning manner, duration, and place are not more difficult than single word adverbs.

However, causality is evidently more difficult to perceive than is time *(34)*. Compare a) "He died of poisoning." with b) "He died in the forenoon." Although the lexical item in sentence (a) is easier than in sentence (b), the causal adverbial makes (a) more difficult *(8)*.

Like adverbial phrases, adverbial clauses involve semantic questions with the additional complexity of adding a whole sentence. Syntactically, adverbial clauses look more difficult than adverbial words and phrases because of the length and the sentence structure. What really causes difficulty seems to be the meaning of some of the subordinating conjunctions. Stoodt *(31)* found that a significant relationship exists between reading comprehension and the comprehension of conjunctions.

UNDERGRADUATE STUDENTS

A second study similar to the first was made using Thai undergraduate students who passed the entrance test to Kasetsart University, Bangkok, Thailand. All of them took the Department of Language English Placement Test. Their scores on the Writing Ability Subtest, rather than on the Structure Subtest, were chosen for analysis because the Structure Subtest checked only the students' recognition of small grammar points, while the Writing Ability Subtest tested their recognition of the whole sentence structure.

The Writing Ability Subtest contained thirty incomplete sentences. The students chose one out of four alternatives to complete each sentence. Only the knowledge of English structure helped them to complete the sentences correctly. The data were collected by taking every third answer sheet from among 1,600 participants. There were 533 altogether.

The obtained correlation coefficient was .64, which was somewhat higher than obtained when testing graduate students [t (531) = 19.2, $p < .001$].

The finding was in accordance with that of Thammongol *(33)* who found a relationship between Thai students' skill in English grammar and effectiveness of expression and their ability to read. She found correlation coefficients of .62 for arts students and .64 for engineering students.

The results of the two pilot studies revealed that syntax affected reading comprehension of the Thai undergraduate students more than graduate students. However, replication is still needed to confirm these findings.

In general, Thai students' reading comprehension appears to depend, to some degree, upon the type of syntactic structure of the printed language. Specific implications include the following.

1. Reading instruction of Thai students (and possibly of other nonnative speakers) will be more effective if the students are taught to analyze the various English structures and to understand the relationship of the various lexical items in such structure.

2. Students should be made aware of the redundancy of language structure.

3. Students should be taught to predict what they will read on the basis of their knowledge of English syntax. Cloze passages might be a promising tool to force students to make predictions about what might be "seen" in the blank.

4. Careful consideration of the relative syntactical difficulty of the textbooks is needed.

5. Simplified texts should be used as a bridge to more difficult reading materials because simplified texts are written with controlled vocabulary and simple syntax.

The writer's pilot study on the relationship between the Thai students' ability to interpret syntactic structure and their ability to comprehend reading passages revealed an unexpected result: The obtained correlation coefficient of .54 for graduate students was not high, although it had been expected that these nonnative speakers of English would rely much on syntax when they read.

However, the writer could not say that this study was completely reliable because it was not planned in advance. The writer collected the available data and made use of the difficulty index of each item, together with her own experience as an English teacher teaching at the college level, to identify the syntactic structure that causes reading difficulty.

The writer will use this pilot study as a guide to conduct another experiment. The future study will be designed to determine which types of structures most affect reading comprehension, regardless of semantic factors, and to what degree they affect it. Ten types of structure will be selected, based on the findings of this study.

So far, the conclusion can be made that syntax does to some extent affect Thai students' comprehension of English passages.

References

1. Botel, M., J. Dawkins, and A. Granowsky. "A Syntactic Complexity Formula," in W.H. MacGinitie (Ed.), *Assessment Problems in Reading*. Newark, Delaware: International Reading Association, 1973, 77-86.
2. Chomsky, N. *Syntactic Structures*. The Hague: Mouton, 1957.
3. Clark, H.H. "Some Structural Properties of Simple Active and Passive Sentences," *Journal of Verbal Learning and Verbal Behavior,* 4 (1965), 365-370.
4. Coleman, E.B. "The Comprehensibility of Several Grammatical Transformations," *Journal of Applied Psychology,* 48 (1964), 186-190.
5. Coleman, E.B. "Improving Comprehensibility by Shortening Sentences," *Journal of Applied Psychology,* 46 (1962), 131-134.
6. Coleman, E.B. "Learning Prose Written in Four Grammatical Transformations," *Journal of Applied Psychology,* 49 (1965), 332-341.
7. Coleman, E.B., and J.P. Blumenfeld. "Cloze Scores of Nominalizations and Their Grammatical Transformations, Using Active Verbs," *Psychological Reports,* 13 (1963), 651-654).
8. Dawkins, J. *Syntax and Readability*. Newark, Delaware: International Reading Association, 1975.
9. Delancey, Robert. "Awareness of Form Class as a Factor in Silent Reading Ability," unpublished doctoral dissertation, Syracuse University, 1962.
10. Evans, Ronald V. "The Effect of Transformational Simplication on the Reading Comprehension of Selected High School Students," *Journal of Reading Behavior,* 5 (1962-1973), 273-281.
11. Evans, Ronald V. "A New Look at Sentence Factors in Readability," *Florida Reading Quarterly,* 10 (January 1974), 8-11.
12. Fagan, William T. "Transformations and Comprehension," *Reading Teacher,* 25 (November 1971), 169-172.
13. Fodor, J.A., and M. Garrett. "Some Syntactic Determinants of Sentential Complexity," *Perception and Psychophysics,* 11 (July 1967), 289-296.
14. Gibbons, H.D. "Reading and Sentence Elements," *Elementary English Review,* 18 (February 1941), 42-46.
15. Glazer, Susan M. "Is Sentence Length a Valid Measure of Difficulty in Readability Formulas?" *Reading Teacher,* 27 (February 1974), 464-468.

16. Goodman, K.S., and J.T. Fleming (Eds.). *Psycholinguistics and the Teaching of Reading.* Newark, Delaware: International Reading Association, 1969.
17. Hamilton, Helen W., and James Deese. "Comprehensibility and Subject-Verb Relations in Complex Sentences," *Journal of Verbal Learning and Verbal Behavior,* 10 (1971), 163-170.
18. Hatch, Evelyn. "Research on Reading a Second Language," *Journal of Reading Behavior,* 6 (April 1974), 52-61.
19. Hittleman, Daniel R. "Seeking a Psycholinguistic Definition of Readability," *Reading Teacher,* 26 (May 1973), 783-789.
20. Hunt, K.W. "Recent Measures in Syntactic Development," *Elementary English,* 43 (November 1966a), 732-739.
21. Hunt, K.W. "A Suggested Measure of Sentence Difficulty," *Florida Reading Quarterly,* 2 (March 1966b), 3-13.
22. Hunt, K.W. "A Synopsis of Clause-to-Sentence Length Factors," *English Journal,* 54 (April 1965), 300-309.
23. Mehler, J. "Some Effects of Grammatical Transformations on the Recall of English Sentences," *Journal of Verbal Learning and Verbal Behavior,* 2 (1963), 346-351.
24. Nurss, J.R. "Children's Reading Syntactic Structures and Comprehension Difficulty," unpublished doctoral dissertation, Columbia University, 1966.
25. Nurss, J.R. "Oral Reading Errors and Reading Comprehension," *Reading Teacher,* 22 (1969), 523-527.
26. O'Donnell, Roy C. "The Relationship between Awareness of Structural Relationships in English and Ability in Reading Comprehension," unpublished dissertation, George Peabody College for Teachers, Nashville, 1961.
27. O'Donnell, Roy C. "A Study of the Correlation between Awareness of Structural Relationships in English and Ability in Reading Comprehension," *Journal of Experimental Education,* 31 (March 1963), 313-316.
28. Ojemann, R.H. "The Reading Ability of Parents and Factors Associated with Reading Difficulty of Parent Education Materials," *University of Iowa Studies in Child Welfare,* 8 (1934), 11-32.
29. Schlesinger, I.M. *Sentence Structure and the Reading Process.* The Hague: Mouton, 1968.
30. Smith, Frank. *Understanding Reading.* New York: Holt, Rinehart and Winston, 1971.
31. Stoodt, Barbara. "The Relationship between Understanding Grammatical Conjunctions and Reading Comprehension," *Elementary English,* 49 (April 1972), 502-504.
32. Strom, Ingrid. "Does Knowledge of Grammar Improve Reading?" *English Journal,* 45 (1956), 129-233.
33. Thammongkol, Kanda. "The English Reading Ability of Thai Undergraduate Students," unpublished paper presented at the Ninth Regional Seminar, SEAMEO Regional English Language Center, 1974.
34. Vygotsky, L.S. *Thought and Language.* Cambridge, Massachusetts: The MIT Press, 1962.

The Image of Foreign Born Persons in Recent Fiction Published in the United States for Children between the Ages of Four and Eight

M. Jean Greenlaw
University of Georgia
Athens, Georgia
United States of America

> We hear about human nature being the same the world around, and in a certain sense this is true, of course: people everywhere fall in love, have friends, mourn their dead, rejoice over births, laugh, cry, despair, and hope. But in many ways there are profound differences that it seems to me we ought to be aware of if we are ever going to understand people of other cultures. And on a globe that seems to shrink daily, that understanding becomes almost a matter of life and death.

This statement by Corcoran *(3)* reflects a concern felt by some about the quality and quantity of books available for children in the United States—books that represent cultures other than that of the United States.

In an attempt to further recognition of books representing other cultures, the American Library Association established the Mildred L. Batchelder Award in 1966 and presented the first award in 1968. This award is presented to an American publisher for a children's book considered to be the most outstanding of those books originally published in a foreign language in a foreign country, and subsequently published in the United States. There is a dearth of books in this category, however. Sawicki *(6)* attributes this to a reluctance on the part of librarians to purchase for children books that are foreign in spirit, tone, or setting. She states that purchase records of translated children's books show that those that are evocative of the American spirit sell, while those that are felt to be truly foreign, don't sell.

The question then becomes, "Are books available to children that illuminate other cultures, or are there merely books that stereotype those cultures in a way acceptable to the purchasing United States audience?" This question generates cause for concern if one believes that literature does influence children's attitudes and values. Studies *(2,5,7)* have shown that this is the case, and it is the belief of this writer that children are affected by what they read.

This study, then, is an attempt to determine whether there is a difference between American and non-American writers of fiction in their portrayal of characters in settings other than the United States.

METHOD

Sample. The Bulletin of the Center for Children's Books was selected as the review medium from which to choose books for this study. This publication of the University of Chicago Graduate School reviews both critically and in depth more books than any other single source. It is widely respected and consulted, gives both favorable and unfavorable reviews, and publishes a suggested age/grade range for books.

The five year period of 1970-1976 (Volumes 24-29) was chosen as the most representative of books of recent times. The books were fiction and fell in the grade range of preschool through third grade. Books had to be two years within that grade range. For example, books classified as grades two to four would be accepted since two of the years were within the acceptable range.

All books reviewed that had a setting outside the United States, written by American and non-American authors were recorded. Ratings by the reviewer did not influence the selection. The nationality of authors was verified by contacting the publishers of each book recorded.

The final sample consisted of all books written by non-American authors (12) with an equal number of books randomly selected from the total number of books written by Americans (17). Therefore, the final sample consisted of 24 books.

Procedure. Content analysis was selected as being the most appropriate method of determining stereotypes presented in children's books. Content analysis, as defined by Berelson (*1*), is the objective, systematic, and quantitative description of the manifest content of communication. The success of a content analysis is dependent upon the selection of the categories. For that reason, the categories used by Gast *(4)* in his landmark study on stereotypes in children's literature were employed.

Data Analysis. Chi-square was used as the measure of analysis and the level of significance was set at .05. The Yates Correction formula was used on all 2 X 2 analyses. The phi coefficient was used to determine the magnitude of association for all significant X^2 values.

RESULTS

The use of chi-square to determine significance of difference in treatment of characters in foreign settings as depicted by American and non-American authors resulted in the following.

No significant differences were found between American and non-American authors on the basis of positive explicit and positive implicit concepts represented in the books analyzed. No significant differences were found between American and non-American authors on the basis of negative explicit and negative implicit concepts represented in the books analyzed. This is shown in Table 1.

Table 2 shows that there were no significant differences in the representation of adults and children as major or minor characters by American and non-American authors in the books analyzed.

Table 3 shows that no significant differences were found between American and non-American authors on the basis of the number of males and females represented as major and minor characters in the books analyzed.

There was moderate, significant (p<.05) association between the economic status of the main characters and whether or not the author was American or non-American. Approximately 25 percent of the variation in economic status can be explained by knowing whether or not the author was American or non-American. Apparently, American authors tend to represent major characters as poor

Table 1
X² for Positive and Negative Concepts in Books

	Non-American	American	X^{2*}	P	$\emptyset$
Positive Concepts					
Explicit	7	5	.29	n.s.	—
Implicit	7	10			
Negative Concepts					
Explicit	8	6	.18	n.s.	—
Implicit	13	16			

df = 1

*Calculated with Yates Correction

Table 2
X² for Age of Major and Minor Characters

	Non-American	American	X^{2*}	P	$\emptyset$
Major Characters					
Child	11	12	.38	n.s.	—
Adult	2	1			
Minor Characters					
Child	7	3	1.68	n.s.	—
Adult	11	17			

df = 1

*Calculated with Yates Correction

more often than do non-American authors. Also, it appears that American authors represent major characters with adequate economic status less often than do non-American authors. A moderate, significant ($p < .01$) association between the economic status of minor characters and the nationality of authors was found. Approximately 33 percent of the variation in economic status of the minor characters can be accounted for by knowing the nationality of the author. Apparently, American authors tend to represent minor characters as poor more often than non-American authors do. Also, non-American authors tend to represent their minor characters as having an adequate income more often than American authors (see Table 4).

Table 3
X² for Sex of Major and Minor Characters

	Non-American	American	X^{2*}	P	$\emptyset$
Major Characters					
Male	8	8	0	n.s.	—
Female	5	5			
Minor Characters					
Male	12	11	.16	n.s.	—
Female	6	9			

df = 1
*Calculated with Yates Correction

Table 4
X² for Economic Status of Major and Minor Characters

Economic Status	Non-American	American	X^{2*}	p	$\emptyset$
Major Characters					
Poor	1	7			
Adequate	9	4	6.62	.05	.50
Comfortable	3	2			
Minor Characters					
Poor	0	10			
Adequate	14	7	12.42	.01	.57
Comfortable	4	3			

df = 2
*Cramer's Phi

Table 5 shows there was a moderate, significant ($p < .05$) relation between educational level and the nationality of the author of the book. Approximately 27 percent of the variation in educational level can be accounted for by knowing the nationality of the author of the book. Apparently, American authors tend to represent major characters with a low educational level more often than do non-American authors. A moderate, significant ($p < .01$) association between the educational level of the minor characters and the nationality of the authors was found. Approximately 27 percent of the variation in education can be accounted for by knowing the nationality of the author. Apparently, American authors tend to represent their minor characters as having little education more often then do non-American authors. Non-American authors tend to represent their characters as having a normal or average education more often than do Americans.

In Table 6 we see that there was a moderate, significant ($p < .01$) association between the social class of the major character and whether or not the author was American or non-American. Approximately 37 percent of the variation in social class of the character could be accounted for by knowing whether or not the author was American or non-American. Apparently, American authors tend to represent major characters as in a low social class more often than do non-American authors.

There was a moderate, significant ($p < .01$) association between the social class of the minor characters and the nationality of the author. Approximately 26 percent of the variation in social class can be accounted for by knowing the nationality of the author. Apparently, American authors tend to represent minor characters as being in a lower social class more often than do non-American authors.

Table 5
X^2 for Educational Level of Major and Minor Characters

Educational Level	Non-American	American	X^{2*}	p	$\emptyset$
Major Characters					
Uneducated	1	8			
Normal	9	5	6.29	.05	.52
College	0	0			
Minor Characters					
Uneducated	2	12			
Normal	13	8	10.09	.01	.52
College	2	0			

df = 2
*Cramer's Phi

Table 6
X^2 for Social Class of Major and Minor Characters

Social Class	Non-American	American	X^{2*}	p	$\emptyset$
Major Characters					
Low	1	9	7.96	.01	.55
Middle	12	4			
Minor Characters					
Low	2	12	7.73	.01	.45
Middle	16	8			

df = 1
*Calculated with Yates Correction

As shown in Table 7, there is a moderately high, significant ($p < .01$) association between the race of the major character and the nationality of the author of the book. Approximately 39 percent of the variation in the race of character can be accounted for by knowing if the author was American or non-American. Apparently, non-American authors tend to represent their major characters as Caucasion more often than do American authors. American authors tend to represent major characters as Black more often than do non-American authors. There was a large, significant ($p < .001$) association between the race of the minor characters and the nationality of the author. Approximately 55 percent of the variation in race can be accounted for by knowing the nationality of the author. Apparently, non-American authors tend to represent their minor characters as Caucasion more often than Americans, and Americans tend to represent minor characters as Black more often than non-American authors.

In the following tables it is shown that all associations are non-significant.

All associations between personality traits of major and minor characters and the nationality of the author were found to be non-significant.

All associations between goals and values of major and minor characters and the nationality of the author were found to be non-significant.

Table 7
X^2 of Racial Group for Major and Minor Characters

Racial Group	Non-American	American	X^2*	p	Ø
Major Characters					
Caucasian	11	3			
Black	2	8	10.18	.01	.63
Oriental	0	2			
Minor Characters					
Caucasian	16	3			
Black	2	13	20.9	.001	.74
Oriental	0	4			

df = 2
*Cramer's Phi

All associations between the positive or negative position of major and minor characters and the nationality of the author were found to be nonsignificant.

All associations between the Katz and Braley Verbal Stereotypes of major and minor characters and the nationality of the author were found to be nonsignificant.

DISCUSSION

If one believes, as this writer does, that children's values and attitudes are affected by what they read, then this study gives cause for concern. We live in a pluralistic society and in a world that daily becomes smaller. It is necessary for us to develop an understanding of cultures that are not like ours. But it seems that there is a minimum of books available that depict other cultures, and those that do exist tend to present stereotype characters.

Of the approximately 3,500 to 5,000 books reviewed in the *Bulletin of the Center for Children's Books* in the selected five year period, only twenty-nine were set in non-American settings and written for children ages four through eight. This seems to be a very small number particularly when we consider that the most impressionable ages are those of the young child.

Table 8
X² for Personality Traits of Major and Minor Characters

Personality Traits	Major Characters					Minor Characters				
	Non-American	American	X²*	p	∅	Non-American	American	X²*	p	∅
Introvert Extrovert	3 10	5 8	.18	n.s.	—	9 9	9 11	.00068	n.s.	—
Authoritarian Democratic	8 5	5 8	.6	n.s.	—	10 8	15 5	.85	n.s.	—
Optimist Pessimist	11 2	11 2	0	n.s.	—	15 3	14 6	.34	n.s.	—
Secure Insecure	12 1	7 6	3.12	n.s.	—	13 5	12 8	.2	n.s.	—
Selfish Unselfish	3 10	4 9	0	n.s.	—	4 14	3 17	.02	n.s.	—
Dependable Undependable	9 4	9 4	0	n.s.	—	14 4	18 2	.036	n.s.	—
Honest Dishonest	12 1	12 1	0	n.s.	—	17 1	20 0	.004	n.s.	—
Infantile Mature	8 5	7 6	0	n.s.	—	6 12	6 14	.014	n.s.	—

df = 1
*Calculated with Yates Correction

Table 9
X² Goals and Values of Major and Minor Characters

	Major Characters					Minor Characters				
	Non-American	American	X^2	p	∅	Non-American	American	X^2	p	∅
Social acceptance in dominant culture	1	0				3	3			
Acceptance own culture	7	3				10	10			
Social advancement	2	0				5	5			
Economic advancement	0	3				4	7			
Self-realization	12	3	9.78	n.s.	–	5	6	.64	n.s.	–
Independence	10	7				6	8			
Future-past orientation	0	0				0	0			
Security	12	9				6	17			
Stability	7	6				12	12			

df = 8

Table 10
X² for + or - Position of Major and Minor Characters

Position	Non-American	American	X^{2*}	p	$\emptyset$
Major Character					
Positive	58	48	1.4	n.s.	—
Negative	7	12			
Minor Character					
Positive	71	81	.017	n.s.	—
Negative	19	25			

df = 1

*Calculated with Yates Correction

Table 11
X² of Katz and Braley Verbal Stereotypes of Major and Minor Characters

Verbal Stereotypes	Non-American	American	X^{2*}	p	$\emptyset$
Major Characters					
Positive	37	37	3.1	n.s.	—
Negative	26	27			
Minor Characters					
Positive	50	57	.5	n.s.	—
Negative	39	33			

df = 1

*Calculated with Yates Correction

American authors writing about non-American settings tended to write about characters as being poor, of low educational level, of low social class, and as being non-Caucasian, particularly Black. Though the stories presented characters in a positive way, they were certainly stereotypic of the "native" of other cultures. Children exposed to these books, representative of the few available, will come away with an unconscious stereotype of inhabitants of other countries being poor, uneducated, of low social class, and Black.

Non-American authors writing about non-American settings tended to write about Caucasian, middle-class people. These authors were British (6), Swedish (2), German (2), Dutch (1), and Swiss (1) and were writing about children in their own cultures.

The implications seem to be that if we are to provide books for children that adequately represent various cultures, we will have to encourage the writing and translation of those books by members of those cultures. Americans writing about other cultures seem to stereotype the characters, and the only available books by non-Americans seem to be those by European authors. Added to those by Europeans should be a variety of books set in other cultures of the world.

This is not to say that all books for children should represent middle-class situations. It is only to say that a variety of cultural settings should be shown, as is true of books set in America.

The encouragement of production of books that accomplish this is a goal that many organizations must contribute toward. Authors must be encouraged to write and publishers must be encouraged to publish these books. The greatest task lies with teachers, however, who must be encouraged to seek out and utilize in classrooms, books that are representative of the societies of the world.

References

1. Berelson, Bernard. *Content Analysis in Communication Research.* New York: Free Press of Glencoe, 1952.
2. Broderick, D. M. "Study in Conflicting Values," *Library Journal,* 91 (May 1966), 2557-2564.
3. Corcoran, Barbara. "Barbara Corcoran." Information Brochure. New York: Atheneum Publishers, 1976, 2.
4. Gast, David Karl. "Characteristics and Concepts of Minority Americans in Contemporary Children's Fictional Literature," unpublished doctoral dissertation, Arizona State University, 1965.
5. Lewis, Isabel Rogers. "Some Effects of the Reading and Discussion of Stories on Certain Values of Sixth Grade Pupils," unpublished doctoral dissertation, University of California at Berkley, 1968.
6. Sawicki, Norma Jean. "The Fate of Translated Children's Books," *Horn Book,* 50 (June 1974), 260-262.
7. Shirley, F. "The Influence of Reading on Adolescents," *Wilson Library Bulletin,* 43 (November 1968), 256-260.

A Comparison of Realistic Contemporary Fiction by Non-American and American Authors for Children Nine through Twelve Years of Age

Shelton L. Root, Jr.
University of Georgia
Athens, Georgia
United States of America

The primary purpose of this study was to discover what differences, if any, there were between works of contemporary realistic fiction by non-American and American authors whose books have settings other than the United States, whose major characters are not citizens of the United States, and which are appropriate for children nine through twelve years of age.

The problem seems an important one since there is common agreement that what children read has the potential for influencing their beliefs, understandings, and attitudes.

What if American children are reading only fiction by American authors—fiction which deals with non-American characters in non-American settings? Will they get biased impressions? Might it not be better for American children to read this type of fiction if it is written by non-American authors? Before such questions can be answered satisfactory, we need to find out what the similarities and differences are between these two categories of books.

METHOD

Sample. The *Bulletin of the Center for Children's Books (1)*, was selected as the review medium from which to choose books appropriate to this study. The *Bulletin* is widely respected and consulted and reviews more children's books in depth than any other single source. The reviews suggest appropriate age and/or grade ranges, and indicate whether a particular book is recommended for young readers. Since this study was not primarily concerned with literary quality, all books reviewed, regardless of recommendation, were included in the initial list of titles from which the final sample was taken.

To represent recent fiction, those books were selected which were published in the United States from 1969 through 1975 and reviewed in Volumes 24 through 28 of the *Bulletin*. From approximately 4,000 titles, both fiction and nonfiction, 35 were found to be appropriate: 24 by American authors and 11 by non-American authors. Ten books from each category were randomly selected for the final sample. Since the *Bulletin* usually suggests an age/grade range of three or four years, only those books were included whose suggested range fell within at least two years of the age group under consideration (ages ten through thirteen would be appropriate as would be eight through ten).

Procedure. Content analysis was selected as an appropriate method for determining certain differences between the two categories of books under investigation. The instruments and categories employed by Gast *(2)* in his study of stereotypes in children's literature were deemed suitable for the purposes of the present study and so employed.

Data analysis. Chi-square (X^2) was used as the measure of analysis and the level of significance was established at .05. The Yates correction formula was used on all 2 x 2 analyses. The Phi ($\emptyset$) coefficient was used to determine the magnitude for all significant X^2 values.

Table 1
X^2 Positive and Negative Concepts

Concepts	Non-American	American	X^2*	p	$\emptyset$
Positive					
Explicit	17	20			
Implicit	27	30	.006	n.s.	-
Negative					
Explicit	9	5			
Implicit	6	5	.007	n.s.	-

df = 1
*Calculated with Yates Correction

Table 2
X² for Age of Major and Minor Characters

Age	Non-American	American	x^2*	p	Ø
Major					
Child	14	12	0	n.s.	-
Adult	0	0			
Minor					
Child	6	8	.25	n.s.	-
Adult	27	22			

df = 1
*Calculated with Yates Correction

Table 3
X² for Sex of Major and Minor Characters

Sex	Non-American	American	x^2*	p	Ø
Major					
Male	10	10	.06	n.s.	-
Female	4	2			
Minor					
Male	17	20	.93	n.s.	-
Female	16	10			

df = 1
*Calculated with Yates Correction

Table 4
X² for Economic Status of Major and Minor Characters

Status	Non-American	American	x^2	p	Ø*
Major					
Low	1	10			
Adequate	5	1	15.4	.001	.77
Comfortable	8	1			
Minor					
Low	7	10			
Adequate	17	9	2.79	n.s.	-
Comfortable	9	10			

df = 2
*Calculated with Cramer's Phi

Table 5
X^2 for Education Level of Major and Minor Characters

Education Level	Non-American	American	x^2	p	Ø
Major					
Uneducated	0	2			
Average	11	7	3.06	n.s.	-
Above Average	2	3			
Minor					
Uneducated	3	2			
Average	21	20	.16	n.s.	-
Above Average	7	7			

df = 2

Table 6
X^2 for Social Class of Major and Minor Characters

Class	Non-American	American	x^2	p	Ø*
Major					
Lower	0	9			
Middle	9	2	16.09	.001	.79
Upper	5	1			
Minor					
Lower	10	8			
Middle	18	15	.68	n.s.	-
Upper	5	7			

df = 2

*Calculated with Cramer's Phi

Table 7
X^2 for Racial Group of Major and Minor Characters

Ethnic	Non-American	American	x^2	p	Ø
Major					
Black	0	0			
Caucasian	11	3	7.73	n.s.	-
Oriental	0	1			
Other	3	8			
Minor					
Black	2	0			
Caucasian	28	13	17.61	.001	.53
Oriental	0	4			
Other	3	13			

df = 3

Table 8
X² for Goals Valued by Major and Minor Characters

Goals	Major Characters					Minor Characters				
	Non-American	American	X^2	p	∅	Non-American	American	X^2	p	∅
1. Acceptance in dominant culture	7	5				2	9			
2. Acceptance in own culture	4	1				6	2			
3. Social advancement	0	0				3	1			
4. Economic advancement	0	2	15.98	.05	.45	5	3	7.21	n.s.	-
5. Self-realization	8	9				7	12			
6. Independence	7	3				5	6			
7. Future-past orientation	0	7				8	10			
8. Security	10	6				19	10			
9. Stability	3	8				15	12			

Table 9
X² for Personality Traits of Major and Minor Characters

Trait	Major Characters					Minor Characters				
	Non-American	American	X²*	p	Ø	Non-American	American	X²*	p	Ø
Introvert Extrovert	3 11	3 9	.6	n.s.	-	8 24	8 22	.02	n.s.	-
Authoritarian Democratic	3 11	4 8	.6	n.s.	-	19 14	17 13	.03	n.s.	-
Optimist Pessimist	9 5	11 1	1.4	n.s.	-	24 9	21 9	.002	n.s.	-
Secure Insure	9 5	5 7	.57	n.s.	-	23 10	21 9	.06	n.s.	-
Selfish Unselfish	0 14	3 9	1.9	n.s.	-	11 22	9 21	.0001	n.s.	-
Dependable Undependable	13 1	11 1	.4	n.s.	-	26 7	27 3	.75	n.s.	-
Honest Dishonest	14 0	11 1	.006	n.s.	-	25 8	27 3	1.34	n.s.	-
Infantile Mature	4 10	2 10	.06	n.s.	-	8 25	6 24	.01	n.s.	-

df = 1

*Calculated with Yates Correction

Table 10
X² for Positive and Negative Characteristics
of Major and Minor Characters

Position	Non-American	American	χ^2*	p	∅
Major					
Positive	67	59	.12	n.s.	-
Negative	3	1			
Minor					
Positive	110	111	5.44	.05	.13
Negative	55	29			

df = 1
*Calculated with Yates Correction

Table 11
X² for Positive and Negative Stereotypes
of Major and Minor Characters

Stereotype	Non-American	American	χ^2	p	∅
Major					
Positive	57	50	.003	n.s.	-
Negative	13	10			
Minor					
Positive	105	105	2.33	n.s.	-
Negative	60	40			

Analyses of the tables yield the following information and, in most instances, raise relevant questions.

Positive and Negative Concepts (Table 1). Even though statistical treatment did not reveal significant differences between non-American and American authors, is it not probable that concepts, either explicit or implicit, revealed through positive characters have more influence on young readers than do concepts revealed through negative characters?

Age of Major and Minor Characters (Table 2). Even though statistical treatment did not reveal significant differences between non-American and American authors, it is noted that both non-American and American authors employed children exclusively as major characters, while both showed a marked preference for adults as minor characters. Is it not possible that at least some books should cast adults as major characters?

Sex of Major and Minor Characters (Table 3). Even though statistical treatment revealed no difference between non-American and American authors, it is noted that both have a proclivity for casting boys as major characters, and that American authors prefer minor male characters over minor female characters by a ratio of 2:1. Is it not time for males and females to receive equal attention in literature for young readers?

Economic Status of Major and Minor Characters (Table 4). Statistical evidence indicates a highly significant difference between non-American and American authors. While a large majority of non-American authors dealt with major characters of adequate and comfortable economic status, most American authors portrayed major characters as being of low economic status. If children were to read exclusively either non-American or American authors, might they not receive unbalanced impressions of cultures other than American? Also, it is noted that non-American authors portrayed well over half of their minor characters as being of adequate or comfortable economic status. If young readers were to read such books exclusively might they not draw erroneous inferences concerning the economic status of cultures other than American?

Education Level of Major and Minor Characters (Table 5). Although there are no statistical differences between non-American and American authors, it is noted that both have strong tendencies to portray both major and minor characters as having average educations for the circumstances in which they are cast. Would children not profit from books which reveal to a greater extent characters from both extremes of the educational spectrum?

Social Class of Major and Minor Characters (Table 6). Statistical treatment reveals that books by non-American authors were far more likely to portray major characters as being of middle or upper social class than were those by American authors who indicated a marked preference for major characters from the lower social class. While not statistically significant, the same tendency is indicated in the treatment of minor characters. Are not both treatments equally, though obversely, distorted? Might not young readers who are exclusively exposed to either group of authors be subject to erroneous impressions concerning the cultures portrayed?

Further, a comparison of Tables 4 and 6 implies a strong relationship between economic and social status with some relationship to level of education (Table 5). Are real life situations as often comparable? Might not children profit from books which reveal examples in which such strong links do not exist?

Ethnic Groups of Major and Minor Characters (Table 7). While there is no difference in treatment of major characters between non-American and American authors, there is a modest statistical difference between the offerings of minor characters. Non-American authors showed a marked preference for minor Caucasian characters, while American authors had a greater tendency for populating their stories with minor characters from the group classified as Other (Australian Aborigine, Lapp, Mediterranean, Mexican, and Mexican Indian). In the cases of both groups, might not young readers profit from books whose major and minor characters reveal a broader assortment of racial origins?

Goals Valued by Major and Minor Characters (Table 8). While no statistically significant differences are indicated in the goals valued by major characters, it is interesting to note that only American authors showed concern over "future-past orientation." Perhaps, because of a longer history, non-American authors are more inclined to take this goal for granted. In the case of minor characters, there seem to be no important differences.

Personality Traits of Major and Minor Characters (Table 9). Both non-American and American authors portrayed their major characters similarly. A composite major character would probably have the following attributes: extrovert, democratic, optimist, unselfish, dependable, honest, and mature. Minor characters would fare in about the same fashion.

Positive and Negative Characteristics of Major and Minor Characters (Table 10). There were no statistically significant differences between non-American and American authors concerning either major or minor characters. However, it is interesting to note that both groups portrayed their major characters as being almost totally devoid of negative characteristics. Is it not quite possible that children of the age for which these books are suggested are ready for and need books which reveal major characters with a more natural balance of positive and negative characteristics?

The more nearly even treatment of minor characters is largely attributable to the fact that many of them were purposely cast by the authors as antagonists. The statistical treatment employed could not analyze the degree to which this is true.

Positive and Negative Stereotypes of Major and Minor Characters (Table 11). Although no statistically significant differences are revealed between the two groups, it is evident, as in Table 10, that positive factors far outweigh negative factors in the case of major characters with a ratio of nearly 5:1. It is speculated that this fact may be the result of the commonly accepted practice of authors using stereotypes to quickly define characters.

Again, as was the case with Table 10, the smaller ratio of positive to negative stereotypes is accounted for by the fact that many minor characters were intentionally cast by the authors as antagonists. Although the statistical procedures employed do not verify this conclusion, an examination of the raw data indicates that antagonists, without exception, were portrayed as having many negative aspects and almost no positive virtues. Again, as with Table 10, the question is raised as to whether young readers are not in need of having even negative characters revealed with some redeeming virtues?

SUMMARY

1. These findings and queries are in some ways influenced by the limitations of the investigator's knowledge of the people, settings, and circumstances revealed in the books under consideration, as well as by his own unidentified cultural biases.

2. The descriptors used to arrive at the findings indicated by Tables 10 and 11 may not have been ideal for the purpose of this study. Descriptors specifically selected for a study of this type might have yielded somewhat different results.

3. Because of the limited universe (37 in approximately 4,000) from which the books for this study were selected, it seems fair to question whether American children have at their disposal enough realistic fiction that is contemporarily set in places other than the United States and whose major characters are not natives of the United States.

4. Because of the frequently marked similarities between books by non-American and American authors, there seems room for valid speculation that most books by foreign authors are selected for publication in the United States because they are, indeed, much like those by American authors.

5. The subjective evaluation by this researcher of the literary merits of the books involved in this study, both by non-American and American authors, is low in most instances.

References

1. *Bulletin of the Center for Children's Books,* Volumes 24-28. The University of Chicago Graduate Library School, University of Chicago Press.
2. Gast, David Karl. "Characteristics and Concepts of Minority Americans in Contemporary Children's Fictional Literature," unpublished doctoral dissertation, Arizona State University, 1965.

PART TWO

Reading in Different Countries and Languages

Most studies in Part Two are descriptive. John Downing, a pioneer in the area of comparative reading, begins the discussion with a statement about the aims and achievements of comparative reading to date. Rigorous, well controlled, cross-cultural research is the ultimate aim. At present, however, descriptions of practices also have a contribution to make. The studies which follow amply bear out Downing's contention. A good case in point is Malmquist's survey of research on reading in Sweden.

One issue raised by Malmquist in his survey is that Swedish data demonstrate conclusively that poor readers are not a sharply distinct group, suffering from a specific physical disability. On the contrary, Swedish researchers "found a relatively smooth and continuous gradation from the poorest readers of the grade to the best." Thus, differences between poor and medium readers were not questions of differences in kind but rather of differences in degree. If one remembers that Japanese reading experts maintain there are no cases of reading failure among normal children in Japan (4), and that in Israel drastic revisions in teaching strategies resulted in a sharp decline in rates of failure which had been very high before (1,2,3), the notion of organically caused learning disabilities in beginning reading is thrown wide open to serious questioning and reexamination, and may become untenable.

Liu's and Leong's separate descriptions of initial processes in learning to decode Chinese, and their efforts to compare them to processes activated in learning to decode English, are further valuable examples of the insights gained as a result of high quality descriptive material.

Abhari's international survey of provisions for producing easy-to-read materials for adult new-literates concludes Part Two.

References

1. Adiel, S. "Reading Ability of Culturally Deprived First Graders," *Megamot (Behavioral Sciences Quarterly)*, 15 (1968), 345-356 (Hebrew).
2. Adler, C., and R. Peleg. *Evaluating the Outcome of Studies and Experiments in Compensatory Education*. Jerusalem: Hebrew University of Jerusalem, 1975 (Hebrew, mimeographed).
3. Feitelson, D. "Israel," in J. Downing (Ed.), *Comparative Reading*. New York: Macmillan, 1973.
4. Sakamoto, T., and K. Makita. "Japan," in J. Downing (Ed.), *Comparative Reading*. New York: Macmillan, 1973.

General Principles of Comparative Reading

John Downing
University of Victoria
Victoria, British Columbia, Canada

In this time of rather rapid growth of interest in comparative reading, it seems appropriate to make sure that the basic principles underlying this new area of study are kept in view.

First of all, let us reiterate the chief aim of comparative reading. It is to apply the methods of cross-cultural research and comparative study in order to achieve a better theoretical and practical understanding of the fundamental psychological processes of literacy behavior, both in their learning and in their developed functioning. This central aim can be furthered in many ways. Progress is not restricted to large scale, cross-national surveys of the IEA type (*10*). Some of the most interesting recent comparative reading studies have been on quite a small scale and some have been conducted inside a single country. Useful comparisons can be made of cultural and linguistic groups living in the same country. Whether the comparative reading research takes place within one country or across national boundaries is not important. The essence of comparative reading studies is that they compare the reading behaviors of people in different cultures and in varying languages in ways which will reveal the fundamental psycholinguistic processes of reading and writing and the ways in which these develop.

At this present early stage in the development of comparative reading research, it is important to retain flexibility in methodology. Open-ended techniques will be valuable because they leave us free to discover the important variables in the natural educational environment. Too rigid an adherence to the traditional methods of testing and measurement of the western world may produce misleading results. For example, conventional social breakdowns of the population may not be applicable, test items may be perceived differently from one culture to another, past testing experiences may be different, and so on. We can learn a great deal about these methodological problems from the know-how which has been painstakingly built up by our colleagues specializing in cross-cultural research in psychology. It would be a valuable contribution to comparative reading if a reading researcher would write a book reviewing and applying the knowledge from cross-cultural research in psychology to our developing methodology of study.

SOME INSIGHTS FROM COMPARATIVE READING

Meanwhile, we are already finding the positive value of comparative reading investigations. Let us consider a selection of examples of ways in which comparative reading is providing new insights into the ways in which children learn to read.

Traditional views on sex differences in reading attainments are having to be reconsidered because of comparative reading research. My own study of learning to read in several different cultures revealed that, whereas girls are superior to boys on average in reading in the primary grades in the United States, this is not a universal characteristic. In England, many studies have found no significant differences between the attainments of girls and boys. In Germany, Nigeria, and India, studies have reported boys to be superior to girls in their average reading attainments. More recently, using the same reading test in four countries, Johnson (5) obtained higher mean scores for girls than for boys in Canada and the United States; in England the difference between the sexes was equivocal; and in Nigeria the boys were ahead of the girls. Currently, a new comparative reading investigation is testing the hypothesis that such sex differences in achievement have their source in cultural stereotypes about the different social roles of boys versus girls. These studies of sex differences provide an example of the insight gained from discovering that patterns of achievement are different from one country to another.

Sometimes insight is gained from finding that the same problem recurs over and over again from one culture or language to another. For example, my own comparison of learning to read in fourteen countries found that a frequent cause of reading problems is using a different language of instruction from the child's mother tongue. Studies in Ireland, Mexico, and Sweden have produced strong evidence that where there is a mismatch between the child's language and the language of instruction massive confusion arises and serious retardation is likely to occur in the development of literacy skills. Further evidence that the child's understanding of the task of learning to read is inhibited by such linguistic mismatches has been reported recently from studies in Canada *(3)*, Greece *(1)*, and Uruguay *(4)*. These findings point to the great importance of cognitive clarity in learning to read. The child's understanding of the linguistic concepts involved in literacy acquisition appear to be just as important as his understanding mathematical concepts in acquiring numeracy.

On this same issue, we can cite an example of a small scale comparative reading study within a single country which provided evidence of the importance of the child's understanding of the task of learning to read. Marie Clay *(2)* compared three cultural groups in Auckland, New Zealand. These were: 1) "Pakehas"—the majority White population; 2) the native Maoris; and 3) immigrants from Pacific Islands—notably Western Samoans. She found several interesting differences but, in particular, the Samoans made better progress than did the Maoris in learning to read in the early years. Clay's perceptive investigation found that the cause lay in the Samoan child's superior understanding of the purposes of literacy. This understanding was derived from frequent experiences of being read to from the Bible, and from observing the high value placed on written communications between their parents and relatives. The Maori children did not have such experiences.

Another example of valuable comparative reading research within a single country is provided by the studies of Sumiko Sasanuma and his colleagues in Japan *(6,7,8,9)*. In this case, the comparison is within a single culture and a single language. This is possible because everyday Japanese written or printed language employs a combination of two kinds of scripts which are quite different in their coding basis.

Kana characters are visible symbols, each of which represents a syllable of Japanese spoken language. In contrast, Kanji characters are visible symbols for morphemes of the Japanese language. Sasanuma has been investigating the differences in impairment of the ability to use these two kinds of script by aphasic patients. The main finding of general interest for reading specialists around the world is that the processing of the two kinds of script can be impaired relatively independently of each other in different types of aphasia. This suggests that there may be two distinctively different modes of operations of linguistic behavior in reading: 1) semantic processing and 2) phonological processing. The Japanese language provides an unusual opportunity to investigate these two different processes, but the findings may be relevant to learning to read in all languages.

These have been just a few examples of the special insight into the psycholinguistic processes of reading and learning to read which is provided by comparative reading research.

References

1. Charis, Constantine P. "The Problem of Bilingualism in Modern Greek Education," *Comparative Education Review*, 20 (June 1976), 216-219.
2. Clay, Marie M. "Early Childhood and Cultural Diversity in New Zealand," *Reading Teacher*, 29 (January 1976), 333-342.
3. Downing, John. "Bilingualism and Reading," *Irish Journal of Education*, in press.
4. Garcia de Lorenzo, Maria Eloisa. "Frontier Dialect: A Challenge to Education," *Reading Teacher*, 28 (April 1975), 653-658.
5. Johnson, Dale D. "Sex Differences in Reading Across Cultures," *Reading Research Quarterly*, 9 (1973-1974), 67-86.
6. Sasanuma, Sumiko, and Osamu Fujimura. "Selective Impairment of Phonetic and Nonphonetic Transcription of Words in Japanese Aphasic Patients: Kana Versus Kanji in Visual Recognition and Writing," *Cortex*, 7 (1971), 1-18.
7. Sasanuma, Sumiko, and Osamu Fujimura. "An Analysis of Writing Errors in Japanese Aphasic Patients: Kanji Versus Kana Words," *Cortex*, 8 (1972), 265-282.
8. Sasanuma, Sumiko. "Kanji Versus Kana Processing in Alexia with Transient Agraphia: A Case Report," *Cortex*, 10 (1974), 89-97.
9. Sasanuma, Sumiko, and Hisako Monoi. "The Syndrome of Gogi (Word-Meaning) Aphasia," *Neurology*, 25 (July 1975), 627-632.
10. Thorndike, Robert L. *Reading Comprehension Education in Fifteen Countries*. Stockholm: Almqvist and Wiksell. New York: John Wiley and Sons, 1973.

Reading Research and the Teaching of Reading in Sweden

Eve Malmquist
University of Linköping
Linköping, Sweden

School administrators and political decision-makers in Sweden now seem to be fully aware of the important role that appropriate reading skills play in all educational activities as unsurpassed learning instruments and also what a general good reading ability means for an increase of the human resources which are available for scientific, intellectual, economic, social, political, and individual progress.

Reading research, nowadays more than ever before, is met with greater interest, acceptance, and respect by school administrators and political decision-makers in Sweden. This does not mean that the influence of reading research as regards the reshaping of our educational system, its organization, its teaching and learning strategies, and its instructional materials is as far reaching and rapid as we researchers would like it to be. The state in Sweden is far from ideal in this respect. But the growing insights of the value of reading research for the improvement of the teaching of reading is nevertheless encouraging and gratifying, indeed.

Swedish researchers within the field of reading have focused their interests mainly in the following areas: beginning reading instruction, reading disabilities, preschool education, reading readiness, language development during preschool and the comprehensive school, measuring instruments, prevention of reading disabilities, and functional reading ability among youths and adults.

READING INSTRUCTION
AND INDIVIDUAL DIFFERENCES

According to the objectives stated in the Swedish school law, the school has to stimulate each child's personal growth toward his development as a free, self-active, self-confident, and harmonious human being. The school must give individual education.

Investigations of first grade children in Sweden *(3)* uncovered a range from 4 years and 11 months to 11 years and 8 months in mental age, while differences between the children's chronological ages were very small (7 years ± 3 months).

A great range of ability in other variables at school entrance was also noted in another experimental study *(6)*. Several children in the population studied (N=386) had very little knowledge of the letters in their own names; 2 to 3 percent knew all the small letters; 80 percent could not read a single word in an easy prose test for the first grade; and 1 to 2 percent reached a standard equivalent to that of the beginning of third grade reading level. Under such circumstances, one cannot justify teaching all children on the assumption that all need the same kind of teaching. Most teachers recognize the great differences between children and within children as to various capacities, background experiences, and personality traits.

To a greater extent now than previously, a diagnostic approach and individualization in teaching are stressed. Steps to further this have included the following:

1. Class size has been reduced to a maximum of twenty-five pupils in the first three years of schooling.
2. The practice of having the child start school at the age of seven has continued, but a certain flexibility as to beginning age is allowed.
3. Better opportunities than before are available for individual tutoring, small-group teaching, teaching in clinics, special classes of various kinds, and special teachers to assist the regular teacher in the classroom
4. Another procedure that has contributed significantly to the individualization of teaching is the division of the class into halves for a certain number of hourly sessions a week for teaching reading, writing, and mathematics in the first three

grades and biology, chemistry, physics, and English and other languages (including Swedish) in the higher grades. This means the teacher has no more than thirteen students at a time (often no more than eight to ten) during ten hours of the child's weekly schedule of twenty hours.

FACTORS RELATED TO READING DISABILITIES

In recent years, the leading specialists in reading have emphasized time and again that only rarely can reading disabilities be ascribed to a single causal factor. Usually, it is a question of a whole complex of factors which may be interrelated with each other and with reading disabilities. It is not always possible, however, to determine the relationship between cause and effect.

Investigations were extensive in Sweden some years ago as regards factors related to reading disabilities in the first grade of elementary school *(3,4,5)*. A relatively large number of factors were studied in the same population and at the same test sessions. Many variables were studied, not only in isolation but also in interaction with other variables, by the use of analysis of variance technique of higher order (multifactorial design).

Out of more than forty variables investigated, the following factors were found to be most intimately related to reading disabilities in the first grade and, further, to most clearly differentiate the group of poor readers from the group of good readers.

1. Intelligence, ability to concentrate, persistence, self-confidence, and emotional stability of the child.
2. Visual perception as measured by five visual perception tests.
3. Social status and educational level of the parents and reading interests in the home.
4. Teaching experience of the teacher as measured by number of years of service in the profession.

By using the case analysis approach, it was found that children with "special reading disabilities" (normal intelligence and very low reading ability) deviated negatively, in a very marked manner, from the mean for the total population investigated, with regard to several other variables besides reading ability. Reading disabilities at first grade level were never isolated defects; in all the cases investigated, they were found to exist together with deficiencies, disturbances, or unfavorable conditions in several other areas.

DO THE POOREST READERS REPRESENT A UNIFORM GROUP WITH REGARD TO THE TYPE OF ERRORS IN ORAL READING?

Medical science often maintains that qualitative differences exist between the various types of errors in reading made by normal readers and those by childrn who are "wordblind," suffering from dyslexia or minimal brain damage, and children with "reading disabilities of some other type."

In my studies I was unable to find any facts in support of the medical hypothesis that, among poor readers, there exists a specific group which can be clearly differentiated and which suffers from a special form of disease; and, moreover, that the qualitative character of the errors in reading made by this group differs from that of other groups of children with reading disabilities or even of normal readers. All conceivable types of errors in oral reading were found among good readers also, although to a much smaller extent. Our data demonstrated conclusively that the poorest readers were not differentiated from the others as a specific, sharply delimited group. On the contrary, we found a relatively smooth and continuous gradation from the poorest readers of the grade to the best. Thus, on the distribution curve for the reading tests used, it was not possible to determine where the best of the poor readers ended and the worst of the medium readers began *(3,4,5)*.

Consequently, it is never a question of actual differences in essence between poor readers and medium readers, but of differences only in degree. In Sweden, therefore, we use an operational definition of the concept of reading disabilities.

CAN READING DISABILITIES BE PREVENTED?

I have reported on a six-year longitudinal study *(6)*, showing that it is possible to markedly decrease the frequency of reading disability cases through a careful diagnosis and a subsequent teaching situation synthesizing ongoing diagnosis and treatment for those who could be expected to experience difficulties judged from the results of a special reading readiness test battery. The pilot study comprised twenty classes with a total of 386 pupils, and the field experiments of seventy-two classes with a total of 1,653 pupils from twelve cities (followed in grades one through three). We used the experimental control group method.

The differences between the groups were studied by analysis of covariance and other methods. A series of multiple regression and correlation analyses were made in order to study the predictive power of various predictors of reading and writing ability in grades one through three. The reading readiness variable consistently had the highest predictive power—between 58 and 86 percent of the combined predictive power of the three predictors—regardless of the criterion variable concerned. In five cases out of six, significant group mean differences supported the hypothesis, as did the occurrence of a region of significance demonstrated by a method of matched regression estimates. Starting from an operational definition of specific reading disability, it was found that more than four-fifths of the cases identified as potential cases of reading disability were prevented from occurring.

LANGUAGE DEVELOPMENT AND SOCIAL INFLUENCE

In his doctoral dissertation, "Language Development and Social Influence," Erasmie (1) studied the language development of a group of 180 children during the years 1963-1972. When the first investigation was carried out, the children were preschool age (4 to 6½ years of age). When the same children were studied in 1972, they were 13 to 15½ years of age and had reached grades six to eight in the comprehensive school. Erasmie's investigation left some interesting results regarding the relationships between linguistic abilities and social background.

From his studies, Erasmie has come to the conclusion that "the school in Sweden of today is to a very minor extent able to achieve the objective of giving all children, irrespective of social background, the same opportunities for education. My results which only concern the development of language, indicate furthermore that the school contributes to increasing the differences in linguistic ability between pupils with different types of social backgrounds."

Erasmie states that his results unambiguously point to the fact that the privileged subjects have been influenced positively, while those belonging to a low social group or having parents with a low education have been influenced to a less satisfactory degree by the school. He is quite aware of the fact that there are factors other than the school influencing the individuals during the nine years they spend in school. "It would be naive to think that the school in itself could elminate differences having to do with socioeconomic circumstances. I feel that it is perfectly clear, that the school has failed to develop sufficiently the linguistic ability of the underprivileged" (1:181).

In other words, the results presented by Erasmie show that the gap in linguistic ability between pupils from different socioeconomic groups, contrary to the objectives, is deepened during the years in Swedish schools.

EFFECTS OF INDIVIDUALIZED READING INSTRUCTION IN PRESCHOOL

Previous research gives us reason to assume that special reading disabilities, to no small extent, are due to some form of sociocultural handicap (e.g., a verbally and intellectually meager childhood environment). Insofar as this is true, early identification of pupils in need of special auxiliary tuition and training of verbal skills must be highly important. I have, therefore, during a three-year longitudinal project studied the effect of individualized reading and writing instruction for six-year-olds at nursery school as compared with ordinary preschool activities not including reading and writing instruction. This effect has been studied with reference to the development of the pupils' reading and writing skills up to the end of grade three of the comprehensive school (7).

The experience gained from a one-year pilot experiment with regard to the children's interest in mastering the subject matter and their ability to do so was of a highly positive nature. The material for exercises to stimulate reading readiness and for the actual practice of reading and writing, with a slowly rising level of difficulty and methodology, especially adapted for children at this mature stage, was found to work satisfactorily. Both material and methodology could, therefore, be applied in the main study, following minor adjustments and additions.

The main study involved 32 groups, each numbering about 10 six-year-old children in five preschools. The various groups at each school were made as equivalent as possible on the basis of the results of some of the basic tests employed (school maturity test, reading readiness test for beginners 1-5/Malmquist/, visual perception 2/Engwall-Malmquist/). Half the groups were then selected by lot to be experimental groups, the remainder being designated control groups. Twelve classes (275 pupils) were selected from grade one classes set up in Linköping comprehensive schools. The pupils in these 12 classes who had attended nursery school the previous year constituted a second control group of the survey.

Four qualified and experienced primary school teachers were appointed for the entire school year to teach the E-group pupils reading and writing during their year at nursery school for two 30-minute lessons daily throughout the school year. Apart from these lessons, the E-group pupils took part in the regular nursery school activities led by preschool teachers.

This is the very first systematic study made in Sweden, including the teaching of reading and writing to six-year-old children. The results of the investigations show that by an early identification of potential reading failures and by a conscious stimulation of language development and a cautious individualized teaching of reading and writing at a low speed, the number of pupils needing special remedial reading in reading clinics and remedial reading classes was greatly diminished during the first three years in the comprehensive school (around 45 percent reduction).

The early start in learning to read and write was found to be of special importance for verbally handicapped children, coming from an environment where adults seldom speak to the children and the conversation is limited in extent and variety. The slow speed in the preschool training gave them fair opportunities to succeed in acquiring the necessary background of meaningful concepts, a sufficiently large vocabulary, ability to listen attentively and to speak reasonably well.

The experimental group children were superior to the control group children at practically all intelligence and maturity levels at the end of the first grade. The effects of the early training in reading and writing according to the used model were found to remain through grades two and three, although the differences between the test results of the two groups were getting smaller.

READING DEVELOPMENT AT AGES SEVEN TO NINETEEN

Recently, Hans Grundin reported on a research project (2) aimed at describing the development of reading, writing, and other communication skills among students aged seven to eighteen years in the Swedish schools.

Since a truly longitudinal study was deemed unfeasible, data were obtained by means of testing simultaneously samples of students from each of the twelve grades involved. A longitudinal element was introduced in that the testing was repeated after one year, using exactly the same tests. This made possible analyses of actually observed rates of progress at each grade level. In order to facilitate comparisons between age groups several years apart, each test was used at as many grade levels as possible. About 2,600 students were tested twice with test batteries including some ten different reading and writing tests.

Only a few of the most interesting results can be pointed out here. There seems to be a continuous increase in the skills studied throughout the school years—except for students in vocational courses in the upper secondary school, where stagnation and even regression in grade eleven are quite common.

The typical growth curve for the total age interval (seven to nineteen years) is negatively accelerated. The growth speed is highest in grade one and then it diminishes with increasing grade level. The development of reading and writing skills is studied for various subgroups of students: for normal learners versus intellectually backward learners, for different socioeconomic strata, etc. On the whole, the differences between subgroups in performance level, which exist after the first school year, tend to remain constant or increase only moderately during the comprehensive school years. There is no indication that the school has the effect of closing or diminishing the gaps between student groups at different performance levels. High performers in the first grades continue to be high performers through the grades and low performers similarly remain low performers. The size of the differences in performance level is reported to be considerable in many cases. The performance level of the bottom 10 percent in grade nine, for instance, is not higher than the average level in grade three.

Grundin discusses to what extent students leaving grade nine of the comprehensive school or different courses in the upper secondary school are functionally literate, i.e., whether they have reached the minimum level of reading and writing skills necessary for their future "functioning" in society.

When discussing reading ability and illiteracy (in international circles, such as Unesco) grade level of reading ability has been used as a criterion of what is called functional literacy. Such a criterion is, of course, unreliable and unsatisfactory for many reasons. A fourth grade level of reading ability does not mean the same in various parts of the world. In some countries, the students are nine years of age when finishing the fourth grade and in others (for instance, Sweden), they are eleven years old.

The time devoted to the teaching of reading and the quality of the instruction vary from country to country. We are probably not too chauvinistic when assuming that the average reading ability of Swedish students at the end of grade four is rather high in comparison with the reading performance level reached in many other countries, where the availability of teachers and instructional materials is worse than in Sweden and the teaching groups much larger. This assumption is supported by the results of the IEA investigations on reading comprehension in fifteen countries (8).

But the demands on Swedish citizens as regards reading ability are already higher than the fourth grade level. In the Swedish society of today there is already a need for a minimum level of functional reading ability corresponding to that of an average student after six years in school. For large groups of citizens, a reading ability of that calibre is already insufficient and, in the near future, the demands of a good reading ability will be considerably higher.

In our TV and computer oriented world, the reading and writing skills seem to be more and more important. All prophecies to the contrary have failed so far. According to the results of this study, around 15 percent (12-20 percent on different tests) of the Swedish students leave the comprehensive school without having reached the sixth grade level of reading ability. In other words, they are not able to function in an adequate way in today's Swedish society. These distressing and discouraging facts have created a lively discussion in Swedish mass media as regards the objectives, means, and results of the teaching of reading in Swedish schools.

SOME CONCLUDING REMARKS

Have we, in our eagerness to teach the techniques of reading, neglected the emotional development of the learner, the creation of interest and motivation for reading?

The interest in Sweden has turned more and more toward studies of the individual learner. Diagnostic studies of his ways of learning are made as a beginning to teach him more efficient learning procedures and to stimulate his own wishes to learn and to help him to be as efficient a self-learner as possible. Such an approach is assumed to be of more value for the individual learner than the most sophisticated packages of learning materials.

The teacher's work is considered to be of the utmost importance, but the proportion of direct teaching has diminished and, instead, an increase of diagnostic measurements can be noted as well as an increase of efforts to raise the individual student's self-concept; self-confidence and self-reliance; his selective abilities with regard to tasks of reasonable difficulty; his motivation for the chosen or the given tasks; his positive emotional reactions; in other words, creating within him a willingness to read and to learn and an awareness of the joy of reading and learning.

References

1. Erasmie, Thord. Language Development and Social Influence. Linköping studies in education. Disseration No. 7, Linköping, 1975.
2. Grundin, Hans U. Läs- och skrivförmågans utveckling genom skolåren (The Development of Reading and Writing Skills through the School years), with a summary in English. Liber Läromedel/Utbildningsförlaget, 1975.

3. Malmquist, Eve. Läs- och skrivsvårigheter hos barn. Analys och behandlings-metodik. (Reading and Writing Disabilities in Children.) Lund, Sweden: C.W.K. Gleerups, 1973.
4. Malmquist, Eve, and André Inizan. Les Difficultés d'appendre à lire. Paris: Armand Colin, 1973.
5. Malmquist, Eve, and Renate Valtin. Förderung Legasthenischer Kinder in der Schule. Beltz Verlag, Weinheim und Basel, 1974.
6. Malmquist, Eve. Lässvårigheter på grundskolans lågstadium. Experimentella studier. (Reading Disabilities at the Primary Stage.) Experimental studies, with a summary in English. Research report No. 13 from the National School for Educational Research. Utbildningsförlaget, Falköping, 1969.
7. Malmquist, Eve. "The Effects of Individualized Teaching of Reading and Writing to Preschool Children" (stencil 1976).
8. Thorndike, R. L. Reading Comprehension Education in Fifteen Countries. International studies in evaluation III. International Association for the Evaluation of Educational Achievement. Uppsala, Almqvist & Wiksell, 1973.

Decoding and Comprehension in Reading Chinese

Stella S. F. Liu
Wayne State University
Detroit, Michigan
United States of America

Non-Chinese speakers often regard Chinese language as difficult to learn, particularly the written language. To native speakers, learning Chinese should be no more difficult than the French learning to read French and the Germans learning to read German. One might argue, however, that an English speaking or a European child has to learn only the alphabet—two dozen signs. A Chinese child has to learn two to three thousand different word signs! Reading specialists are aware, nonetheless, of the difficulties letters can create for millions of children and adults alike, at least in the United States. The problems native Chinese readers experience are not known, as no published research from the People's Republic of China is available to this writer. A search into sources published in English has revealed only one study (made in Vancouver, British Columbia) with Chinese speaking children learning to read both Chinese and English (8).

A teacher instructing children to learn a language, even though it is the native language, ought to have clear notions of the nature of the language; the relationship between the spoken and the written aspects of the language; the relationship between words, grammar, and meaning; and the appropriate strategies for learning.

This paper attempts to delineate some of these notions on teaching decoding and comprehension in reading Chinese. The reader is first oriented in the Chinese language from a historical perspective, and guided through a discussion on some theoretical and practical issues.

NATURE OF THE CHINESE LANGUAGE

Stages in Evolution

Of the many characteristics of the Chinese language, the most important is that it is monosyllabic, which means every word consists of one single syllable. Historically, the word or character began as a simple pictographic representation of the object. A "man" marching with two legs was represented by 入 and a "horse" was drawn like this 馬. Thus, from the beginning, a sign indicated a whole word, not by its *sound* but its *meaning*. For three thousand years, pictographic signs have progressed through a process of conventionalization, "horse" through such forms as 馬 and 馬 before settling in its modern form 馬, and "man" has been only slightly modernized to 人. This ideographic essence has remained to this day, with "one" written —, "two" as =, and "three" indicated by ≡.

The second stage of development—still creating a character for a whole word and only for its meaning, not for sound—was to construct a graph by combining two or more already existing simple graphs. A pictograph 介, modernized 宀, for the word "roof," and a pictograph 豕, now 豕, for the word "pig" combined to form the character 家 (chia) the pig under the roof denoting "house," "home," "family." There are many hundreds of such compounds of ideas in Chinese writing. Even so, this scheme did not suffice.

Script inventors began phonetic loaning in the third stage. Homonyms such as "sun" and "son" and "two" and "too" in English were much more numerous in Chinese with its many short monosyllables. There was a word anciently pronounced *ləg which meant "to come." At the same time there was another *ləg (lai) which meant "barley." The latter was written with a pictographc 來. Because it was difficult to draw the abstract *ləg "to come," the graph *ləg "barley" was borrowed for the former. The resulting word "to come" is now 來 (lai). Bolder steps were taken toward borrowing existing graphs for similar sounding words which were abstract and without their own graphs. Thus, 箕 "basket" was loaned to the similar sounding word meaning "his," "their" 其 in modern script. A small number of such cases of borrowing could, of course, not create any great disorder, but in great quantity it might lead to intolerable uncertainty as to what the graphs in the sequence really meant; whether they had their original, concrete meaning, or whether they stood as phonetic loans for something else (7:12). This borrowing method, as it was, had to be improved.

The result was a new and ingenious method in stage four—combining two simple graphs in another way. For example, there existed a pictograph ⼿ *siog (drawing of a hand or five fingers) meaning "hand" and another graph ⼝ anciently read *k'u "mouth." But there was also another word *k'u "to beat." This latter word was made by combining the element "hand" denoting the meaning, i.e. something done by the hand, and the borrowed sound of *k'u "mouth" for the new word 扣 (now 扣) "to beat." Thus, a new kind of compound character was obtained which consisted of a *phonetic* (*k'u "mouth"), a part indicating sound, and a *signific* ("hand"), a part suggesting the meaning. In this way, by combining already existing graphs in pairs, one of which functioned as phonetic and the other as signific, new signs could be devised practically without limit. Hundreds and thousands of such half-ideographic, half-phonetic compounds were created. The result was that nine-tenths of all Chinese characters are constructed according to this principle (7,14).

Structure of the Characters

The two elements making up the great majority of Chinese characters are commonly known as the *radical* and the *phonetic*. The signific or determinative radicals which give meaning to characters are designated as the "Water Radical" 水 (written as 氵), denoting something liquid; the "Tree Radical" 木 (written 朩), evoking the idea of trees or wood; the "Heart Radical" 心 (written 忄), referring to emotions, etc. Radicals are arranged from simple to complex, according to the number of strokes, from one stroke to seventeen. Within each stroke category, each radical has been given a number. For example, in the one stroke category, the radicals from 1 to 6 are –, ｜, 丶, 丿, 乙, 亅, respectively. Examples for six strokes are 竹 (radical 118, "bamboo"), 米 (radical 119, "rice"), 羊 (radical 123, "sheep"), 耳 (radical 128, "ear"), etc.

The Chinese Grammar

Unlike Indo-Europoean languages, Chinese language has no conjugation or inflections. In Chinese writing, each word is immutable, uninflected, and equivalent to a root.

The whole grammar depends on word position. Chinese characters are capable of acquiring all sorts of grammatical values according to the position they occupy in the sentence, or phrase, and according to the words used in conjunction with them. It is the relative position of the words which determines their role, thus giving meaning to expression. The same character 我 (wo, I) can be a subject in 我爱你 (Wǒ, ài nǐ, "I love you") or an object in 你爱我 (Nǐ ài wǒ, "you love me"). It might also mean "we" or "us." None of these changes in meaning would involve any change in the character; rather, they depend entirely on their positions in the sentence.

Furthermore, characters used as verbs may also function as nouns or even as adjectives and adverbs. The character 上 may mean "to ascend" as a verb, "top" as a noun, "upper" as an adjective, besides others. There is a tremendous latitude in which a given character may be used, thus providing a high degree of possibilities for combinations of unit word forms in the language.

Oral and Written Language

The oral language spoken by approximately 94 percent of the Chinese people is the "Han language," which is subdivided into hundreds of dialects. Chinese scholars have organized the dialects into eight major groups *(10:3).*

> Northern Mandarin—occupies a large area in Northern China, in about twelve provinces
>
> Eastern Mandarin—spoken in two provinces
>
> Southwestern Mandarin—spoken in approximately five provinces
>
> Wu dialects—spoken in the East, including Shanghai
>
> Gan-Hakka
>
> Min group—has Northern and Southern subgroups
>
> Cantonese dialect
>
> Xiang group

Aside from the phonological features specific to the groups, there are also lexical items more or less peculiar to each of these groups. Among the various groups, some are mutually unintelligible for speakers who have had no previous speech contact with those groups. The differences between some groups are greater than Spanish and French or even French and Italian (9:11).

On analyzing the sounds of the language, one finds words in Mandarin end either in a vowel or in *n, ng,* or *r,* rather poor in its resources as compared with some other languages, such as English. This meager stock of sounds, however, is compensated by the fact that every word has its own tone as a phonemically distinctive feature. Every syllable carries a tone which also distinguishes lexical meanings. There are four basic tones: high (as in bā "eight"), rising (bá "to uproot"), low (bǎ "to hold"), falling (bà "a harrow") (*16*).

A recent study (*1*:95) using a computer file of 737 dialect locations grouped modern tones into 14 categories. The analysis gives a breakdown of the number of tones found in a certain number of dialect locations.

	Number of Tones	Found in Dialect Locations
Northern Mandarin	3	17
	4	291
	5	38
	6	1
Southwestern Mandarin	4	143
	5	29
	6	30
Eastern Mandarin	5	10
	7	2
Cantonese	6	3
	7	2
	8	2
	9	9
	10	1

It is noted that the majority of the dialects have these four tones: Tone 1A—long, level, low; Tone 1B—lower than Tone 1A; Tone 2—short, level, high; Tone 3—high rising. Within each of the dialect groups, the largest number of tones is either falling or level in tonal contour.

With such vast linguistic diversity, Chinese people would not be able to communicate at all except for a single, unified writing system. Chinese writing styles range from classical writing (which is still being practiced, especially in poetry and literary writing) to modern colloquial writing. Generally, the most common form is a style falling between the formal and the colloquial.

RECENT DEVELOPMENT: LANGUAGE REFORM IN PRC

Character Simplification

Language reform efforts in China up to 1949 were concerned with schemes for alphabetization, but after the establishment of the People's Republic of China (PRC) in 1949, the top priority in language reform was given to character simplification. As early as 1950, a list was published of commonly used simplified characters. Other lists have been developed through the years. Reform extends to abolishing many words (1956), simplifying characters by reducing the number of strokes from an average of sixteen to eight per character (1964), reducing the traditional 214 radicals to 189 (1964), collecting characters simplified by the masses and publishing a dictionary in which newly simplified characters (1973) are included (9:46-57).

Presently, all new publications in the PRC are printed in simplified characters. Only in rare cases are the original characters used, such as in texts for historical studies of the writing system or for calligraphic art purposes. Store signs on the streets are generally in simplified characters, and children are taught simplified characters in school.

Visitors to the PRC often see simplified characters not yet officially approved. Examples of some recently simplified characters follow:

Original	Simplified	Pronunciation	Meaning
餐	歺	cān	"meal"
酒	氿	jiǔ	"wine"
漆	沏	qī	"paint"

The Lehmann report (9:48) noted that "There seems to be a common direction of simplification of characters having many strokes. The direction is to make these characters analyzable into components which are words in their own right or can be pronounced separately." For instance, my second example has 酒 (jiǔ, "wine") as its original. The simplified form retains the 氵 ("Water Radical") giving the meaning for being liquid, but borrows another character 九 (jiǔ, "nine") the phonetic part to form the newly simplified character 氿 (jiǔ, "wine") saving many strokes from 酉 (seven strokes) to 九 (two strokes). For some characters, the phonetic loan component is not homophonous with the original but rhymes with it as the simplified 宔 for 寨.

Thus, the simplification reform seems to follow logical reasoning that marked the trend of character development through its evolutionary stages discussed previously.

Standardization and Use of Putonghua

For purposes of national unity and need for communication, Putonghua普通話 has been declared the common language in the PRC, embodying the pronunciation of the general Peking dialect, the grammar of Northern Chinese dialects, and the vocabulary of modern colloquial Chinese literature (9).

To popularize the standard dialect, training workshops were held for large numbers of people, party, and administrative workers who were instructed to learn to speak Putonghua. Formal meetings are held in Putonghua, and all schools in the nation were asked to use it as the medium of instruction.

Considering the linguistic complexities cited previously, these are commendable achievements. Another significant change in education witnessed by visitors to the PRC is the effort of transmitting the language of everyday life to the classroom. Students go out to interview workers and peasants and record their life experiences. People in the community are brought into the classroom as resources. In areas where local dialects such as Cantonese and Fukinese are very different from Putonghua, any degree of achievement in this aspect is worthy of study.

DECODING AND COMPREHENSION IN READING CHINESE AS THE NATIVE LANGUAGE

The logic of the Chinese script actually makes decoding much less difficult than many instructors have believed. This would be true if the teacher has knowledge of the development himself, and is able to help the student to see the logic of the structure. Such was not the case as recalled by this writer who, as a child, was taught Chinese as a native language in Canton, China many years ago. Learning was done primarily by rote. Characters were memorized by repeatedly tracing strokes on workbooks for the purpose of learning handwriting. The traditional pride that Chinese take in calligraphy demands that children put in long hours of practice with the brush from the beginning of their reading and writing instruction. This visual motor reinforcement undoubtedly facilitates the character acquisition and retention process. When one becomes unsure of the structure of a character or a part of it, it is common for one to attempt to trace it with one or two fingers in the air, on the palm, or on any surface. Indeed, Chinese practiced the kinesthetic method long before Fernald introduced it to disabled readers (or did Fernald learn it from the Chinese?).

Pinyin for Decoding

The teaching of Chinese in the PRC as witnessed by the Lehmann delegation shows considerable change from the traditional practice experienced by this writer. One of the thrusts of the language reform movement is the creation of the pinyin 拼音 alphabetic writing, using Roman phonetization. Pinyin is used to facilitate the learning of characters and to speed Putonghua popularization. Charts for the pinyin system found in the back of Xīnhuá Zìdiǎn 新华字典 , a small dictionary of 85,000 words first published in 1971 in Peking, include the English alphabet in capital and small letters, the consonants, and a table for vowels. In addition to the alphabet letters, the Chinese symbols used in the traditional sound system are given as further aid for pronunciation. The three tables are reproduced below:

The Alphabet

一 字母表

Aa	Bb	Cc	Dd	Ee	Ff	Gg
Hh	Ii	Jj	Kk	Ll	Mm	Nn
Oo	Pp	Qq	Rr	Ss	Tt	
Uu	Vv	Ww	Xx	Yy	Zz	

Consonants

二 声母表

b	p	m	f	d	t	n	l
g	k	h		j	q	x	
zh	ch	sh	r	z	c	s	

Vowels

三 韵母表

	i	u	ü
a	ia	ua	
o		uo	
e	ie		üe
ai		uai	
ei		uei	
ao	iao		
ou	iou		
an	ian	uan	üan
en	in	uen	ün
ang	iang	uang	
eng	ing	ueng	
ong	iong		

Upon entering primary school, usually at age seven (Chinese are counting may be a year ahead of the Western system), and after nursery school and kindergarten, children are taught the written language of Putonghua using pinyin as the first writing system.

The pinyin system is introduced beginning with the names of the consonants, e.g., [puo tə kə]. Then vowels are introduced, followed by the nasal finals, and subsequently the dipthongs. Syllables are learned and analyzed as consisting of two parts, the initial, and the final—an analysis which reflects a long history of Chinese linguistic tradition. For example, a student pronouncing the syllable *hong*, will say something like [xɤ], [ɤŋ], [xɤŋ], the *h* being a voiceless velar fricative (9:55).

In Mandarin speaking areas, about four or five weeks are spent on studying pinyin. In non-Mandarin areas, with strong interference from local dialects, more time is allotted. In Canton, for example, six weeks are needed for the initial presentation of pinyin.

Decoding Characters

After the initial period of instruction of pinyin, characters are introduced. Each character is also given in pinyin. Structure of characters and their component parts are analyzed; basic strokes are identified by name, such as *nà* 捺 for a downward, right-slanting stroke (㇏), *héng* 横, for a horizontal stroke written from left to right (㇐). Numbers one to ten (一二三四五六七八九十) are used in teaching the basic strokes as they embody most of the stroke types used in writing Chinese. Students are further taught popular names for frequent characters or parts of characters from the currently accepted 189 radicals. The character 红 (hong, "red") is analyzed by left and right components, the left being the radical 纟 (sī, silk), and the right 工 (gong) as in 工人 (gōng-ren, worker). The student is thus able to learn a character by its pronunciation, using pinyin, and by its traditional form. Characters having phonetic components naturally are easier to analyze and remember.

By the end of second grade, students learn to spell and pronounce syllables in pinyin and to utilize pinyin in learning new words and correcting local accents. In third grade, students use pinyin in looking up words in the dictionary and in reading simple texts written in pinyin. Fourth grade and upward students read texts in pinyin without difficulty and can transcribe easily. Upon entering junior high, students are expected to have mastered pinyin.

Learning of characters goes on simultaneously with pinyin. On completion of primary school, a student is expected to master about 3,000 basic characters. In composition, if a word is needed for which the character has not been learned, the student is encouraged to write in pinyin.

Information about how much writing is required of students in learning characters is not known. Based on this writer's own childhood experience, it is reasonable to surmise that the traditional writing practice on characters has continued. The value of writing in learning characters has been substantiated by a study made on American beginning students of Chinese at the college level (2). Students in the control group, for whom writing was required, performed better in recognition as well as in production than students in the experimental section who were not required to practice writing. Students in the experimental section who practiced writing a great deal privately did better in recognition than the rest in the same section. Writing and reading characters seem to be associated skills which reinforce each other.

Reading Comprehension and Chinese Speaking Children

Meaning or comprehension in reading can be achieved in two ways: mediated (indirect) and immediate (direct) meaning identification (15:206). Figure 1 illustrates the two pathways.

Path A associates the graphic input with a mediated process, such as word identification through some acoustic image. The meaning of the graph is assessed via the sound image, which serves as an intermediary. Path B leads from the graph directly to its meaning without an intermediary. English orthography is an example that uses path A; Chinese orthography uses path B. Japanese orthography interestingly uses both path A (Kana) and path B (Kanji).

Phonetic orthographies like English seem to have two distinct advantages. One is that the number of sound distinctions in any

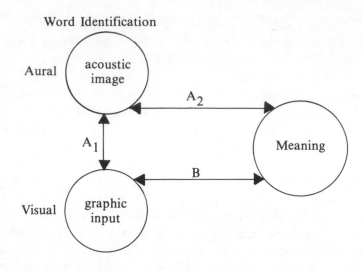

Word Identification

Aural

acoustic
image

A_2

A_1

Meaning

B

Visual

graphic
input

Figure 1. Relation of Orthographies to Meaning.

language is small (under 100) so that the number of symbols to be learned is correspondingly small. The other is that, in principle, once the child has learned the idea of path A, he can read or write anything that is in his speaking vocabulary (*17*).

Orthographies like Chinese have other advantages. One obvious advantage is that Chinese graph can have immediate or direct access to meaning, without the intermediary of sound. The tendency to sub-vocalize has been referred to as "auditory lag" causing reduction of reading speed and hindering comprehension. Since path B does not involve sound, this problem is largely eliminated. Second, people who have trouble forming the path from graph to sound would not face this difficulty. Children who suffer from impairment in speech production need not have this impairment transferred to reading and writing. Third, Chinese characters are "fixed length" codes, each one a neat little square. English words are of variable length, where the length or complexity of the word depends not on its associated meaning but on its sound. This may have important implications on efficiency of eye scanning. Also, a page of Chinese characters contains significantly more information than a page of printed English, since each character, which takes little more space than a letter of the alphabet, comes from a much larger set (*17*).

There is some evidence (Sasanuma, 1974) that the processing of path A and path B involves relatively independent neural mechanisms since Japanese aphasics can be selectively impaired in either Kana or Kanji (the part of Chinese characters). Makita (*11*) has reported that Japanese children have hardly any reading disabilities, in contrast to the situation in the United States. Erickson et al. (*5*), however, provide data that the phonetic associations of Kanji may be stronger than their graphic associations. Rozin et al. (*12*) report success with teaching American children with reading problems to read English represented by Chinese characters.

References

1. Cheng, Chin-Chuan. "A Quantitative Study of Chinese Tones," *Journal of Chinese Linguistics*, 1 (January 1973), 93-110.
2. Chin, Tsung. "Is it Necessary to Require Writing in Learning Characters?" *Journal of the Chinese Language*, Teachers Association, 8 (November 1973), 167-170.
3. Chu, Chauncy C. "The Passive Construction—Chinese and English," *Journal of Chinese Linguistics*, 1 (September 1973), 437-470.
4. Creel, Chang Rudolph. *Literary Chinese by the Inductive Method*, Volume 1. Chicago: University of Chicago Press, 1938, 1948.
5. Erickson, D., I. G. Mattingly, and M. T. Turvey. "Phonetic Activity in Reading— An Experiment with Kanji," *Journal of Acoustical Society of America*, 52 (1972), 132.
6. Herdan, G. *The Structuralistic Approach to Chinese Grammar and Vocabulary*. The Hague: Mouton, 1964.
7. Karlgren, B. *The Chinese Language*. New York: Ronald Press, 1949.
8. Kline, Carl L., and Lee Norma. "A Transcultural Study of Dyslexia: Analysis of Language Disabilities in 277 Chinese Children Simultaneously Learning to Read and Write in English and in Chinese," *Journal of Special Education*, 6 (1972), 9-26.
9. Lehmann, Winfred P. (Ed.). *Language and Linguistics in the People's Republic of China*. Austin and London: University of Texas Press, 1975.
10. Li, Fang-Kuei. "Languages and Dialects of China," *Journal of Chinese Linguistics*, 1 (January 1973), 1-13.
11. Makita, K. "The Rarity of Reading Disorders in Japanese Children," *American Journal of Orthopsychiatry*, 38 (1968), 599-614.
12. Rozin, P., S. Poritsky, and R. Sotsky. "American Children with Reading Problems Can Easily Learn to Read English Represented by Chinese Characters," *Science*, 171 (1971), 1264-1267. (Follow-up on July 16, 1971.)

13. Samuels, S. Jay. "Automatic Decoding and Its Role in Reading Comprehension," *Technical Report*, 4 (March 1973), Minnesota Reading Research Project, University of Minnesota.
14. Simons, W. *How to Study and Write Chinese Characters*. London: Lund Humphries, 1944.
15. Smith, Frank. *Understanding Reading*. New York: Holt, Rinehart and Winston, 1971.
16. Thompson, S. A. *The Chinese Language Today—Features of an Emerging Standard*. Paul Kratochirl. London: Hutchinson University Library, 1968.
17. Wang, William S-Y. "Informal Thoughts on Reading," unpublished manuscript shared with this writer, June 3, 1974.
18. Wrenn, James L. *Chinese Language Teaching in the United States—The State of the Art*, 1968.
19. Xinhua, Zidian. 新华字典 (*New Chinese Dictionary*). Peking: 商务印书馆 1971, 1973.

Learning to Read in English and Chinese: Some Psycholinguistic and Cognitive Considerations

C. K. Leong
University of Saskatchewan
Saskatoon, Saskatchewan, Canada

" 'Did you say *pig* or *fig?*' said the cat. 'I said pig,' replied Alice." That short exchange from Carroll's *Alice's Adventures in Wonderland* illustrates some of the prerequisites in learning to read in English. Alice had to consider the contrastive patterns of stop and continuant consonants in choosing the former while rejecting the latter. In the same speech segment, she also used the gravity and tenseness of /p/ as distinct from the acuteness of /t/ and the laxness of /b/. All these attributes were combined into a bundle of distinctive features (phonemes). The phoneme /p/ was followed by phonemes /i/ and /g/, themselves bundles of simultaneously produced distinctive features. Hence, to discriminate between "pig" and "fig" Alice had to discern and differentiate between the concurrence of simultaneous entities and the concatenation of successive entitites—differentiations important in the learning to read process in English.

As learning to read in English builds on the speech processes of the child, it is largely learning by eye and by ear (*17,18*). Similarly, it is not an oversimplification to say that learning to read in such a disparate writing system as Chinese is largely learning by eye and by hand. Figure 1 illustrates specimen Chinese characters and words. The character 中 meaning "centre," combined with another character 間 gives the equivalent word "middle." The character 醫 (medicine, to cure) has three components meaning: a) wound enclosing

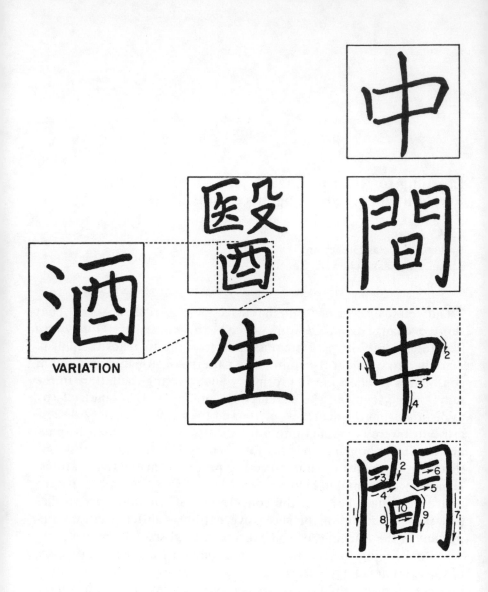

Figure 1. Illustration of an orthography best learned by eye and hand—Chinese. Reading is from right to left, top to bottom. Note the symmetry and rhythm of the characters. Those enclosed in dotted lines also show the flow of the strokes.

ⵧ an arrow 矢 (医); b) extracting foreign bodies with an instrument 殳 ; and c) treating wound with tincture 酉 which is a variant of wine 酒 (tincture diluted with water 氵). The character 醫 in combination with 生 (to give birth or to grow) means a healer, a physician. The illustration of the number and direction of strokes shows the balance and flow of each character—attributes to be mastered by hand. It is therefore, no surprise that beginning readers in Chinese start learning to write early and write much as well. This spaced and massed practice, capitalizing on the eye-hand "linguistic awareness" of the language, must help the learning to read process in Chinese.

All beginning reading is largely the mapping of the encipherment in script, be it English or Chinese, onto some underlying "lexical representation" and meaning. Almost all models of learning to read, particularly of word identification, emphasize reading as an active, analytical, and synthetical process (6,7,8). This involves high speed visual scanning of graphic symbols, analysis of critical features from clusters of letters to progressively higher order units of structure, evocation of some inner thought, and the understanding of syntactical relationships. Within this framework, some researchers (14,28,33,34) have stressed the importance of the phonological representation of beginning reading in an alphabetic system. It is likely that an ideographic system like Chinese will make contact with the inner "lexical representation" more at the morphological and less at the phonetic base. It is the aim of this paper to explore further similarities and differences of the psycholinguistic and psychological processes underlying initial reading in English and Chinese.

OVERVIEW OF ENGLISH AND CHINESE AS SYMBOL SYSTEMS

It is generally agreed that the English orthography with 26 letters of the alphabet and some 46 phonemes is a more efficient system for information processing. Uncertainty among 26 alternatives of the alphabet as given by - log 1/n (or - log 1/2 with two alternatives) is 4.7 bits of information if each letter is regarded as equi-probable, and 4.03 bits if the distributional redundancy is considered (35). If to the 26 letters are added comma, period, space, and a few other punctuation marks, then the information given by any one of the symbols is about 32 (2^5) or 5 bits. There are, however, more than 26 or 32 *functional units* which are critical to reading. One of the tasks the beginning reader has to do is to identify clusters of letters or letter groups, which number some 65 graphemic units according to Venezky in his analysis of a 20,000 word corpus. He explains that the spelling or graphemic units "are not related directly to sound, but to an intermediate (morphophonemic) level first and then to sound (*41*:84). Morphophonemic rules are a complex set of relationships between orthographic symbols and the phonological system of speech. Certain clusters of letters and, hence, phonemes are possible according to these rules but do not actually occur (e.g. "sklig"). On the other hand, the reader should be aware, implicitly or explicitly, that in "mis′ hap" the *sh* does not form a cluster as the two letters are separated by a morphemic boundary (*41*:84). Similarly, *ch* is realized as [č] in "chief," as [š] in "chef," or as [k] in "echo" (*42*:36). "Knowing" these phonological rules will reduce uncertainty (in the information sense) on the part of the reader and will help him in his reading.

In contrast, Chinese is a good example of ideographic or morphemic writing in which each symbol, usually referred to as a character, represents a morpheme. The language is best described as monosyllabic, isolating (compared with inflexional languages), and analytical (with few bound forms) [*16, 21*]. Estimate of the minimum number of characters to be mastered as adequate for practical purposes is from 3,500 characters (*20,21*) to between 4,000 and 7,000 characters (*44*). Assuming a newspaper uses between 4,096 (i.e. 2^{12}) and 8,192 (i.e. 2^{13}) characters, a single character thus gives between 12 and 13 bits of information. This increase in information value compared with the 4 or 5 bits carried by letters of the English alphabet is achieved at the expense of the memory load required. It must also be borne in mind that the basis of a word in Chinese is a combination of two or more characters. The permutation and combination of, say, 4,000 characters usually within the repertoire of a grade six child will thus yield many more usable words at his disposal. In fact, the authoritative Kanghsi dictionary lists from 42,000 to 48,000 characters, depending on the editions referred to, with about 6,000 to 7,000 characters as being actively used. This corpus of active and latent characters may be compared with Oldfield's estimate (*29*) of 75,000 entries as the size of the literate (British) adult.

The noted linguist and sinologist Chao (*1*) lists ten criteria for a good symbol system and concludes that Chinese does not rank very high on these requirements, except in "elegance." This refers to the symmetry of the symbols and the information value per chunk (see Figure 1). As an orthography, Chinese has shown stability over geographical space and historical time as it has served well the Chinese and related language communities (e.g. the Japanese and the Koreans) over thousands of years. The stability reflects much slower structural changes and less susceptibility to dialectical variations than the alphabetic system. The eminent linguist Halle (*13*) makes a rare slip when he refers to the arbitrary symbols of Chinese and rote memory needed in memorizing these characters. The present writer has attempted to dispel this myth and show how the radicals and phonetics composing a character constitute the critical units and resemble morphophonemics in English (*21*). When the linguist Wang claims that Chinese "is not conspicuously complex" and that "it is simpler than the western languages" (*44*:51), he also refers to Chao's criterion of elegance and information value of the characters.

THE WORD

Even though we read in sentences and connected prose with words embedded in context, psychological experiments have shown the value of studying the word and its relation to reading.

In English, a word is usually defined as a morpheme or a combination of morphemes, although meaning can be conveyed in other ways. A word is also defined as a unit of syntax. Operationally, a word is a graphic unit separated by visual spaces with orthographic constraints and intraword redundancies. In Chinese, a word is less easily defined. An individual graphic symbol or character tzù (字 [tsz] unaspirated, falling tone) is at best the sociological equivalent of a word. It is interesting to note that the sinologist Soothill (*40*) deliberately left characters untranslated in his 1899 dictionary, *The Student's Four Thousand* 字 , which some authors correctly translated as *Four Thousand* [*Characters*], while quite a few librarians thought " 字 " in the title was a decoration and left it out altogether in the catalogue! Strictly, a character as the smallest functional unit is a morpheme and corresponds to the syllable in English (*1,19,21,44*). Wang

(43) further notes that the number of strokes (see Figure 1 for illustration of order and geometric position of strokes) in a character approximates the number of letters in an English word and that there is a "parallelism in information content between the stroke and the letter." Moreover, the complexity of a character in terms of the number of strokes bears little relationship to the ease or difficulty in reading or spelling. Leong (21,22) has found from a count of 1,851 commonly used characters that the average stroke number is 11.27 and this compares with the mean of 11.61 with another list of 2,830 characters. There is no evidence from his empirical studies that "simple" characters in terms of number of strokes are easier to learn. The syntactic word in Chinese is t z ú (詞 [t s ʻʐ] aspirated high-falling tone), which is the smallest immediate constituent unit of segmental sentences. The equivalent of the English word "middle" is composed of two characters (see Figure 1) and it should be noted that strings of characters are not separated by visual spaces except at the end of a sentence.

Reference has been made to the role of critical features and the phonological representation in perceiving words. If it is phonemic discrimination which is important to the beginning reader in English, it is tonemic discrimination to the child learning to read in Chinese. A tone is primarily the pitch pattern of the vocalic nucleus of a syllable, which is traditionally divided into an "initial" and a "final." If the initial is voiced, the tone begins with the initial and spreads over the whole syllable. If the initial is voiceless, the tone is spread over the final only. In the national language (Mandarin) there are four tones: high level (₍ヂ), high rising (亠), low rising (夫'), low falling (㇀,). A change in tone alters the meaning of a symbol just as a change in a phoneme would alter the meaning in English. The tone change is illustrated in the schematic oscillographic tracing in Figure 2. It should also be noted that the Chinese language has a large number of vowel sounds and a small number of consonant sounds. The dominant pattern is for one consonant at the beginning of a vowel, except for fricatives (/ts/, /dz/, /ch/, /dj/), which are regarded as single sounds. The final consonants /n/, /ŋ/, /m/, /p/, /t/, /k/ are truncated. Thus, every character or syllable must have a vowel sound or a semi-vowel sound of /n/, /ŋ/, or /m/ but only about two consonant

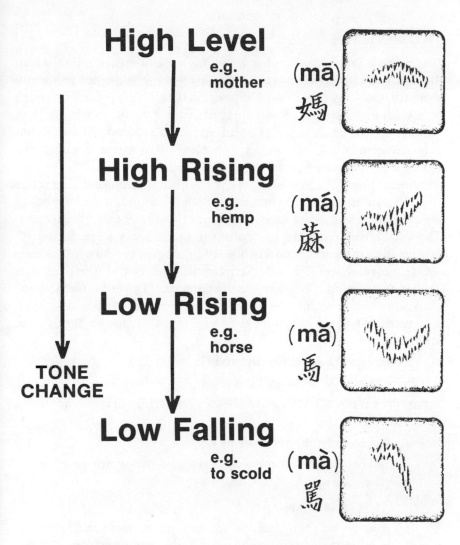

Figure 2. Illustration of tone changes in Chinese with schematic oscillographic tracing.

sounds. The dominance of vowel over consonant sounds leads to a large number of homophones, which are distinguished one from the other by the system of tone changes explained above. Chao has commented that, on the whole, there is "probably no more ambiguity in spoken Chinese than in most other languages spoken" (*1*:75).

THE SENTENCE

Perceiving a word also implies knowing the construction into which the word can enter when words are arranged in sequence to form a sentence. One way to explain a sentence is that it is a free form bounded by pauses at both ends. Some linguists find it useful to use the term "utterance" for an instance of occurrence of a sentence, as significant prosodic elements (pitch, stress, juncture) often affect meaning. An example is: "They *are* (,) starving children" compared with "*They* (,) are starving children." Linguistic awareness underpinning reading refers to both syntactical and semantic knowledge in addition to phonological representation. This is clear from the above pair of sentences. The oft-quoted example of "colorless green ideas sleep furiously" further illustrates this relationship. Phonologically and syntactically the sentence is well-formed. Semantically, it is ill-formed as it is devoid of meaning. The ambiguous sentence, "The girl looked up the road" further explains the need to understand surface and deep structures. The two ways of grouping the sentence to resolve the ambiguity are:

   a. The girl (looked [up the road]).

   b. The girl ([looked up] the road).

A parallel example in Chinese is the two renderings of the same strings of characters:

   a. Ta tzoou (,) bu hao.　　他走 (,) 不好。

      (That he goes is not good—he had better not go.)

   b. Ta tzoou bu-hao.　　他走不好。

      (He cannot walk well.)

The full tone on bu (buh) and the optional pause between "Ta tzoou" and "bu hao" in sentence (a) make it a different sentence from sentence (b) in which "tzoou - bu - hao" is one word with no break. A similar example is the doggerel when different junctures make for different meaning:

   a.　　落雨天留客 (,) 天留我不留 。

      (literal translation - Rainy day retains guest, day [the elements] retains [guest] but I do not retain [guest].)

b. 潮有天 (,) 留客天 (,) 留我不 (,)留 。

(literal translation - Rainy day, day to retain guest; retain me not? retain.)

According to (a) the guest is unwelcome to stay even though it rains; according to (b) a rainy day is just the day to stay! It is thus clear that when the suprasegmental phonemes (including tones) and the prosodic elements are all specified, they help to determine the meaning of a sentence, be it in English or Chinese.

There are, however, some differences in processing sentences in different writing systems. The importance of the potential pause between subject and predicate is reflected in the Chinese usage with regard to punctuation. With the literary style of writing, it is the practice to pause after about four syllables even though there is no punctuation. An example from the classics is:

大學之道 (,) 在明明德. 。

(Free translation - "The way of the great learning [S - Subject], lies in illuminating the illustrious virtues [P - Predicate].") This is in contrast to written English where a subject and a verb are never separated by punctuation.

Another difference is the limited or optional use of anxiliaries in the Chinese sentence. In the Chinese equivalent of the English sentence "His mother spank*ed* him last week" the phrase "spank*ed* him" can be expressed either as "ta - liao t'a" (打了他) or "ta t'a" (打他). More often than not, the presence of anxiliaries is due to rhythmic reasons. Equally puzzling to the beginning reader is the maintenance in interrogative sentences of the same word order as in declarative sentences. The question "Does he come?" where word order is inverted for interrogation can be rendered as "T'a lai pu lai." ("He come(s) not come(s)" or "He comes; he comes not"), or "T'a lai ma?" ("He come(s)?"). In the former sentence, the speaker posits the possible alternatives.

"LINGUISTIC AWARENESS" AND LEARNING TO READ

That different writing systems constrain the reading process differentially can be expected (9). The question is, at what level and to what extent does the beginning reader recode the requisite phonological, syntactical, and semantic representation from the alphabetic or morphemic script? This recording in English goes far beyond the one-to-one grapheme-phoneme correspondence, as would be the case with Morse code ciphers. Chomsky (3:15-16) dismisses this simplistic correspondence as "something of a pseudo issue" and goes on to say:

> What the beginning reader must learn (apart from true exceptions) is simply the elementary correspondence between the underlying segments of his internalized lexicon and the orthographic symbols.

This lexical representation refers to the deeper level and the more complicated relationship than that afforded by the auditory matching of one symbol and one sound. An example is the differential realization of "courage" which is phonetically [kʌ'rəǰ] in isolation and [kərḗyǰ] in the context of "courageous." The vowel reduction to a neutral schwa [ə] is brought about in both renderings by contextual changes and stress shift. The child who distinguishes the two renderings and reads them correctly needs to:

a. respond to the root or lexicon unit of Koraege,

b. modify the pronunciation according to phonological principles, and

c. respond to or modify the phonological principles by his understanding of syntactical rules and the addition of graphemes (e.g. a suffix) to the lexical form.

The English orthography thus preserves the similarity of meaning and signals different usage (and sound) in a way far beyond the simple one-to-one mapping. Decrying the overemphasis of teaching one-to-one phonic correspondence such as teaching "bat" as "b-a-t, buh-ah-tuh, say-it-very-fast, bat" Smith (38:89) goes so far as to say that phonics will provide only "a *clue* to the sound (or 'name') of a configuration being examined. Phonics can provide only approximations."

That the one-to-one letter-to-sound correspondence in English is not adequate to explain initial reading and that the representation of deeper phonological, syntactical, and semantic system is essential are emphasized by various workers. These include linguists such as

C. Chomsky (2) and N. Chomsky (3); psycholinguistic empiricists such as Venezky (41,42); cognitive psychologists such as Gibson (6,7) and her Cornell group (8); and experimental psychologists at the Haskins Laboratories such as Cooper (4), A. Liberman et al. (25), I. Liberman (26), Mattingly (28), and Shankweiler and Liberman (33,34). This latter group, while accepting the psychological realities of the phoneme, has demonstrated that consonants and vowels are not discrete entities in the signal, but are encoded as one overlapping acoustic segment (24). Figure 3 shows the temporal overlapping of initial and final consonants and the all pervasive influence of the vowel. There is no place to dissect the syllable "bag" into the usual portions (as taught in schools) of [b], [æ] and [g]. The continuous restructuring of the message shows phonemes such as /b/ or /g/

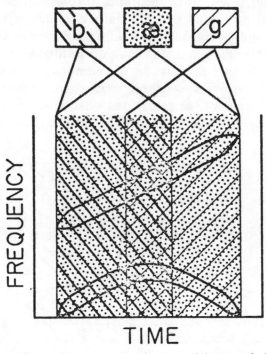

Figure 3. Schematic spectrogram showing parallel transmission of phonetic segments after encoding to the level of sound (after Liberman, 1970).

cannot be isolated but are recognizable only in an acoustic environment. The temporal telescoping of the phonetic string into syllables can be extended into a comparable collapsing of the deep structure into surface structure as represented schematically in Figure 4.

It is from such ongoing theoretical and empirical studies in psychoacoustics that recently Gleitman and Rozin (*10*) advocated the use of the syllable as a unit for initial acquisition of reading. This position has drawn some rather intemperate remarks about the "silly syllables" as "not the units of language" in a critique from Goodman (*12*). Granted that the Rozin, Poritsky, and Sotsky (*30*) experiment showing the successful use of the syllabary with innercity school children suffers from some methodological weaknesses and that the Gleitman and Rozin recommendation of the rebus (with pictures representing concrete words) as a "syllabic curriculum" has limited usefulness and poses other theoretical problems, the fact remains that individual phonemes are only realized in the context of acoustic environment and that segmentation into phonemes by young children is difficult. Segmentation into syllables is posited as an alternative in the learning to read process. In his admonition of Gleitman and Rozin, Goodman overlooks these researchers' important qualification, in a footnote, of the role of the syllable as "neither where the child begins, nor is it where one would want him to end up, in reading;

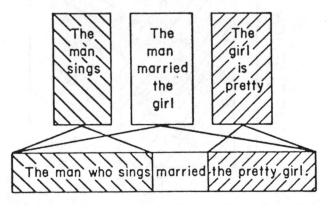

Figure 4. Schematic representation showing parallel transmission of deep structure segments after encoding to the level of surface structure (after Liberman, 1970).

words and phrases are the units with which the child begins . . ." (*10:* 463) and the authors' emphasis on the acquisition of phonological principles. Goodman is right in pointing out that syllabification has its inherent difficulties. For one thing, overemphasis on syllabification goes against the principle of economy of the English alphabet as there are many more syllables than there are letters of the alphabet and phonemes. For another, syllabification is not simply going by "what the sound says" in hyphenation with such results as "drummer" hyphenated wrongly into "drum-mer" where it should have been "drumm-er." Shuy *(36)* outlines some "semiordered syllabification rules"—lexical, grammatical and phonological—to highlight difficulties in defining limits of a syllable.

It should be noted that in speaking of phonological features Jakobson and Halle (*15*:31) seem to be emphasizing the syllable as well:

> The distinctive features are aligned into simultaneous bundles called phonemes; phonemes are concatenated into sequences; the elementary pattern underlying any grouping of phonemes is the syllable.

It is clear that the perception of language (as well as its production) depends on the understanding of distinctive features in phonemes and the concatenation of phonemes into larger clusters such as the syllable. Learning to read builds on a phonetic base. The emphasis of such writers as Goodman (*11*) and Smith (*37*) on meaning almost to the neglect of the link between reading and speech applies more to mature, fluent reading rather than to initial reading. Interestingly enough, when Smith (*39*:350-351) states that "the English spelling system indicates how words are related in meaning independently of their sound," he can be presumed to be referring to the Chinese orthography. Mention has been made of individual Chinese characters being equated with syllables and strokes within characters with letters of the alphabet. Insofar as each character is learned as a "whole" the correspondence to a syllable is evident. The present writer has shown (*21*) that there are invariant spelling-to-morpheme or even to sound units within each character. The phonetic, giving the sound equivalent, and the radical, giving the meaning of a character, constitute the phonemic-semantic constituent so critical to learning to read. An example is the character 染 "dye" which has a sound component not far removed from 九 "pellet" (hence the common misspelling of 染). Morphologically 染 is composed of 氵 "water," 九 "nine" (times), 木 "wood" (a dye stuff in olden days); hence the meaning of the character as a whole. The distinctive properties of the radicals and phonetics in Chinese might be compared with letter groupings in the English morphophonemics. The important point is that understanding of intraword morphemic elements helps beginning reading. This, in the last analysis, is a cognitive process requiring the use of efficient rules and strategies in encoding symbols (22).

In learning to read, the problem of finding the best segment—be it a phoneme, a syllable, a word, or a phrase—cannot be answered without knowing the nature of the task and the linguistic awareness of the beginning reader. Gibson and Levin (8:289) are emphatic:

A *multilevel* approach is essential. What the child reads must make sense. At the same time, it must not be so hard that he fails. Whatever the segment, it must be the most economical one that he is capable of processing.

It is of more than academic interest to explore Luria's claim (27:411) that "the different bases for writing in different languages must entail a different cortical organization." Clinical studies of aphasic Japanese patients with and without apraxia of speech (31,32) seem to show that the Chinese character or Kanji component and the syllabary or hiragana component of Japanese are processed differently in the neural mechanisms. The Kana transcription seems to relate to the "phonological processor" in the brain while the Kanji transcription could bypass such processing. If this is substantiated, the role of the auditory short term store, so important in learning English, will be a diminished one in learning Chinese. Empirical studies with Kanji by the Haskins group (5), and their ongoing research into the relationship between reading and speech (34), point to the importance of the auditory short term store as "necessary to primary linguistic activity" and that morphological information may require phonetic storage at an intermediate stage of processing. The Sasanuma and Fujimura results are interpreted not as independent neural processing of the alphabetic and morphemic components, but as differential realization of linguistic awareness.

References

1. Chao, Y. R. *Language and Symbolic Systems*. Cambridge: Cambridge University Press, 1968.
2. Chomsky, C. "Reading, Writing, and Phonology," *Harvard Educational Review*, 40 (1970), 287-309.
3. Chomsky, N. "Phonology and Reading," in H. Levin and J. P. Williams (Eds.), *Basic Studies on Reading*. New York: Basic Books, 1970.
4. Cooper, F. S. "How Is Language Conveyed by Speech?" in J. F. Kavanagh and I. G. Mattingly (Eds.), *Language by Ear and by Eye*. Cambridge, Massachusetts: The MIT Press, 1972.
5. Erickson, D., I. G. Mattingly, and M. T. Turvey. "Phonetic Activity in Reading: An Experiment with Kanji," *Haskins Laboratories Status Report on Speech Research SR-33*, 1972, 137-156.
6. Gibson, E. J. "Learning to Read," in H. Singer and R. B. Ruddell (Eds.), *Theoretical Models and Processes of Reading*, Second Edition. Newark, Delaware: International Reading Association, 1976.
7. Gibson, E. J. "Ontogeny of Reading," *American Psychologist*, 25 (1970), 136-143.
8. Gibson, E. J., and H. Levin. *The Psychology of Reading*. Cambridge, Massachusetts: The MIT Press, 1975.
9. Gillooly, W. B. "The Influence of Writing-System Characteristics on Learning to Read," *Reading Research Quarterly*, 8 (1973), 167-199.
10. Gleitman, L. R., and P. Rozin. "Teaching Reading by Use of a Syllabary," *Reading Research Quarterly*, 8 (1973), 447-483.
11. Goodman, K. S. "Words and Morphemes in Reading," in K. S. Goodman and J. T. Fleming (Eds.), *Psycholinguistics and the Teaching of Reading*. Newark, Delaware: International Reading Association, 1969.
12. Goodman, K. S. "The 13th Easy Way to Make Learning to Read Difficult: A Reaction to Gleitman and Rozin," *Reading Research Quarterly*, 8 (1973), 484-493.
13. Halle, M. "Some Thoughts on Spelling," in K. S. Goodman and J. T. Fleming (Eds.), *Psycholinguistics and the Teaching of Reading*. Newark, Delaware: International Reading Association, 1969.
14. Huey, E. B. *The Psychology and Pedagogy of Reading*. New York: Macmillan, 1908.
15. Jakobson, R., and M. Halle. *Fundamentals of Language*. The Hague: Mouton, 1971.
16. Karlgren, B. *Sound and Symbol in Chinese* (rev. ed.). Hong Kong: Hong Kong University Press, 1962.
17. Kavanagh, J. F. (Ed.). *Communicating by Language: The Reading Process*. Bethesda, Maryland: U.S. Department of Health, Education, and Welfare, National Institutes of Health, Government Printing Office, 1968.
18. Kavanagh, J. F., and I. G. Mattingly (Eds.). *Language by Ear and by Eye: The Relationships between Speech and Reading*. Cambridge, Massachusetts: The MIT Press, 1972.
19. Kratochvil, P. *The Chinese Language Today*. London: Hutchinson University Library, 1968.
20. Leong, C. K. "A Study of Written Chinese Vocabulary," *Modern Language Journal*, 56 (1972), 230-234.

21. Leong, C. K. "Hong Kong," in J. Downing (Ed.), *Comparative Reading: Cross-National Studies of Behavior and Processes in Reading and Writing.* New York: Macmillan, 1973.
22. Leong, C. K. "Dichotic Listening with Related Tasks for Dyslexics—Differential Use of Strategies," *Bulletin of the Orton Society*, 25 (1975), 111-126.
23. Leong, C. K. "Lateralization in Severely Disabled Readers in Relation to Functional Cerebral Development and Syntheses of Information," in R. M. Knights and D. J. Bakker (Eds.), *The Neuropsychology of Learning Disorders: Theoretical Approaches.* Baltimore: University Park Press.
24. Liberman, A. M. "The Grammar of Speech and Language," *Cognitive Psychology*, 1 (1970), 301-323.
25. Liberman, A. M., et al. "Perception of the Speech Code," *Psychological Review*, 74 (1967), 431-461.
26. Liberman, I. Y. "Speech and Lateralization of Language," *Bulletin of the Orton Society*, 21 (1971), 71-86.
27. Luria, A. R. *Higher Cortical Functions in Man.* New York: Basic Books, 1966.
28. Mattingly, I. G. "Reading, the Linguistic Process, and Linguistic Awareness," in J. F. Kavanagh and I. G. Mattingly (Eds.), *Language by Ear and by Eye: The Relationships between Speech and Reading.* Cambridge, Massachusetts: The MIT Press, 1972.
29. Oldfield, R. C. "Individual Vocabulary and Semantic Currency," *British Journal of Social and Clinical Psychology*, 2 (1963), 122-130.
30. Rozin, P., S. Poritsky, and R. Sotsky. "American Children with Reading Problems Can Easily Learn to Read English Represented by Chinese Characters," *Science*, 171 (1971), 1264-1267.
31. Sasanuma, S., and O. Fujimura. "Selective Impairment of Phonetic and Nonphonetic Transcription of Words in Japanese Aphasic Patients: Kana vs. Kanji in Visual Recognition and Writing," *Cortex*, 7 (1971), 1-18.
32. Sasanuma, S., and O. Fujimura. "An Analysis of Writing Errors in Japanese Aphasic Patients: Kanji vs. Kana Words," *Cortex*, 8 (1972), 265-282.
33. Shankweiler, D. P., and I. Y. Liberman. "Misreading: A Search for Causes," in J. F. Kavanagh and I. G. Mattingly (Eds.), *Language by Ear and by Eye: The Relationships between Speech and Reading.* Cambridge, Massachusetts: The MIT Press, 1972.
34. Shankweiler, D. P., and I. Y. Liberman. "Exploring the Relations between Reading and Speech," in R. M. Knights and D. J. Bakker (Eds.), *The Neuropsychology of Learning Disorders: Theoretical Approaches.* Baltimore: University Park Press.
35. Shannon, C. E. "Prediction and Entropy of Printed English," *Bell Systems Technical Journal*, 30 (1951), 50-64.
36. Shuy, R. W. "Some Language and Cultural Differences in a Theory of Reading," in K. S. Goodman and J. T. Fleming (Eds.), *Psycholinguistics and the Teaching of Reading.* Newark, Delaware: International Reading Association, 1969.
37. Smith, F. *Understanding Reading.* New York: Holt, Rinehart and Winston, 1971.
38. Smith F. *Psycholinguistics and Reading.* New York: Holt, Rinehart and Winston, 1973.
39. Smith, F. "The Relation between Spoken and Written Language," in E. H. Lenneberg and E. Lenneberg (Eds.), *Foundation of Language Development: A Multidisciplinary Approach*, Volume 2. New York: Academic Press, 1975.

40. Soothill, W. E. *The Student's Four Thousand* 字 *and General Pocket Dictionary*. London: Kegan Paul, 1942. (Originally published, 1899.)
41. Venezky, R. L. "English Orthography: Its Graphic Structure and its Relation to Sound," *Reading Research Quarterly*, 2 (1967), 75-106.
42. Venezky, R. L. "Regularity in Reading and Spelling," in H. Levin and J. P. Williams (Eds.), *Basic Studies on Reading*. New York: Basic Books, 1970.
43. Wang, W. S-Y. "Review of Lin: Chinese Characters and Their Impact on Other Languages of East Asia," *Modern Language Journal*, 15 (1971), 187-188.
44. Wang, W. S-Y. "The Chinese Language," *Scientific American*, 228 (1973), 51-60.

Easy-To-Read Materials for Adult Semiliterates: An International Survey

J. A. Abhari
International Institute for Adult Literacy Methods
Tehran, Iran

Adult literacy is considered an important factor in overall individual and community development. We hear more and more of regional and national campaigns against adult illiteracy. Political demands for universal literacy are emerging in most countries of the Third World.

During the past decade great sums of money were allocated for this purpose. Thirty million dollars were spent for Experimental World Literacy Projects, carried out in eleven countries over a period of two to four years. There are no figures available to estimate the cost of such projects in other countries.

The great majority of these adult literacy projects are short, informal programmes. In a survey of 100 adult literacy projects, made by IIALM* in 1971, it was found that the mean duration of the literacy courses was 300 hours. During this time the basic techniques of reading, writing, arithmetic, and, more recently, some functional information about participants' jobs, have been taught. These skills are not developed to the extent of enabling the learner to make independent use of them; for permanent learning, such skills need more practice.

---

*The International Institute for Adult Literacy Methods was established by Unesco and by the Government of Iran in Tehran, in December 1968. The objectives of the Institute are, broadly, to provide documentation, information, research and training services relating to literacy programmes—in particular, methods, techniques, and means used in adult education.

In a Survey of Readers' Interest and Preference in eight villages of Iran, the graduates of literacy classes, in comparison with those who had finished fourth year of elementary education and those who had attended a traditional school, scored lowest in the literacy achievement test.

International and national authorities have expressed their dissatisfaction with the results of these short term adult literacy programmes. It has been realized that the students and the graduates of these programmes are not able to participate fruitfully in the development of their society, or in their own development, which is the objective of the planners and policy makers.

The Unesco Year Book and other international statistical source books do not include statistics on the number who became literate in such programmes.

The organizers of literacy campaigns have realized that the neoliterates do not remain literate for long, and most of them relapse into a state of virtual illiteracy. Thus the time, energy, and money put into literacy teaching is often wasted.

A possible solution to the problem is to make available to the neoliterates an extensive range of attractive and informative follow-up materials on which the basic literacy skills acquired could be easily practiced and reinforced.

Some believe that even before a literacy campaign is started, there must be an appropriate supply of suitable reading materials.

Except for a small number, adult literacy programmes have not envisaged the provision of systematic follow-up activities such as easy-to-read materials. Although the World Congress of Ministers of Education (held in Tehran in 1965) put special emphasis on follow-up programmes, some of the Experimental Functional Literacy Projects which were the outcome of the Congress considered literacy follow-up activities of secondary or auxiliary importance. This weakness was recognized in the Critical Assessment published last year.

Due to the important role follow-up materials play in fostering and retaining literacy skills, the International Institute for Adult Literacy Methods has concentrated its research activities in this field. In a study on reader interest and preference, it was found that availability and accessibility to reading materials were important factors in establishing reading habits. Among the eight villages studied there was one with a library and a publications stand. The semiliterates in this village read more often, spent more money on reading materials, and scored highest in a test which was administered to measure literacy skills.

This Institute also carried out an International Survey of Publishers of Easy-to-Read Materials. A questionnaire directed to the publishers of easy-to-read materials was prepared to collect the information needed for this survey. Among the replies received before the deadline, ninety-five were from publishers who were completely, or at some stage of their work, involved in the preparation of easy-to-read materials for adults, and had answered over 75 percent of the questions.

The publishers who replied to the questionnaire were from all over the world: 17 in Africa, 36 in Asia, 4 in Europe, 5 in North America, and 26 in South America.

I. ORGANIZATION OF PUBLISHERS

a. Type of Organization

In terms of sponsorship, the greatest proportion of the publishers were nongovernmental, making up 62 percent of the total.

Production of easy-to-read materials is carried out mainly by institutions which organize literacy programmes. Fifty-six of the ninety-five responses were from the publication divisions of literacy organizations, and their prime purpose was to prepare the reading materials required or recommended by their main offices. Eighteen were not part of a literacy organization, but had relations with such organizations. There were eleven enterprises who published easy-to-read materials independently of literacy organizations.

b. History of Production of Easy-to-Read Materials

Production of easy-to-read materials is rather recent. Few publishers produced such materials before 1940, and 80 percent of those who answered the questionnaire had become involved in this task within the past fifteen years.

c. *Objectives and Finances of Publishers*

Development of reading skills and growth in reading habits were the most frequently mentioned objectives by both government and non-government publishers. Among other objectives, family life education and entertainment were most frequently mentioned among non-governmental publishers, and expansion of national language was mentioned by the government publishers.

The annual budget of the publishers who responded varied from US $115 to US $2,000,000. There were only seven publishers with an annual budget exceeding US $100,000. Most are allocated $1,000 to $10,000 a year for this purpose.

Publication of easy-to-read materials has not been a lucrative enterprise. Among the respondents, only six publishers indicated that they marketed easy-to-read materials at a profit. There were six others whose loss in this area was balanced by the profit they made in publishing other materials. Three sold materials at printing cost. The rest gave materials free of charge or at a nominal price.

Most of the publishers received some sort of assistance from national or international organizations, the latter being the main source. According to the replies, the international organizations supported government publishers and national sources supported private publishers.

II. PRODUCTION OF EASY-TO-READ MATERIALS

a. *Surveys Carried out by Publishers*

The majority of the publishers realized the importance of preliminary surveys in preparing materials and had sponsored some sort of inquiry in order to obtain the results which would guide them in writing their manuscripts. These studies were usually informal, and not many of them were ever published. Studies undertaken most often related to measurement of reading interest, measurement of reading ability, preference for particular types of illustrations, and word count.

Aside from the results of preliminary studies, there were other criteria for determining the content of the manuscripts. These usually related to the readers' personal and community needs and interests, the reading level and comprehension of the readers and, of course, to the objectives of the publishers.

The respondents used different approaches in evaluating their publications. The most frequently mentioned were: 1) interviewing readers and teachers; 2) empirical field tests; 3) observation of readers' progress in the class; 4) criticism offered by evaluators, critics, and community leaders; and 5) judgments of authors and staff.

b. Type, Content and Language of Publications

The materials published for adult semiliterates were mainly in book form. Other types mentioned, in order of frequency, were: pamphlet, newspaper, magazine, almanac, and encyclopaedia. The range of circulation of different types of materials was very wide. In 1973-1974, press runs ranged from fewer than 1,000 copies to 4,000,000. For 64 percent of the publications prepared by respondents in 1973-1974, fewer than 10,000 copies each were printed.

The areas covered in these materials were, in order of frequency: occupational skills, general information, fiction, family-life education, community education, religion, and popular subjects of interest.

The respondents published easy-to-read materials in 148 different languages: 44 African dialects, 44 Asian languages, 3 European languages, and 57 Latin American languages and dialects.

The majority of the materials published for adult semiliterates in 1974 were in bold letters with black and white illustrations.

III. WRITERS AND THEIR TRAINING

The writers of the materials published were, in order of frequency: staff personnel, school teachers, professional writers, university professors, and new literates. Many publishers solicited the assistance of specialists, such as physicians and technicians, in preparing manuscripts.

Thirty-two publishers employed writers who had had no special training aside from their experience in working with literacy organizations and in teaching literacy classes. The others employed writers who had attended writers' workshops, seminars, or special courses on how to write easy-to-read materials for adults. Writers' guides had been prepared by several organizations.

Finding well-trained writers and willing authors has been the most serious problem encountered.

IV. DISTRIBUTION OF MATERIALS

Literacy projects and teachers were mentioned most frequently as the means of distribution of materials among adults. Other media of distribution mentioned were, in order of frequency: mail, book sellers, libraries, middlepersons, and mobile libraries.

Publishers usually aimed at a national readership and at men. Four respondents published exclusively for readers in urban areas, twenty exclusively for rural readers, and sixty-four for both urban and rural readers. Distribution has been one of the most frequently mentioned problems of the respondents. Slow communication, lack of proper cooperation and incentive among distributors and others involved, and shortages of staff and storage space were among the other problems of distribution.

V. READERS' PROFILE

Graduates and students of literacy classes were the main clients of these publishers. Other readers included school dropouts, regular students, linguistic minorities, and migrants. The offerings of most of the publishers were read by more than one group. The publications of non-government publishers reached a wider range of readers than did government publications. The government publishers concentrated on students and graduates of literacy classes. Among the respondents only the nongovernmental publishers prepared materials for linguistic minorities.

Both types of publishers concentrated more on the rural areas.

VI. PUBLISHERS' PROBLEMS

As mentioned before, finding well-trained and willing authors has been the most frequently recognized problem of publishers in different regions of the world. Other problems relate to the scarcity of basic printing materials, constant increases in the price of paper and of other printing facilities, and distribution costs. Low purchasing power among new literates, the limited size of the market, a lack of cooperation among the institutions involved, absence of scientific research on readers' interests, and lack of illustrators (artists) were other problems noted.

VII. COMMENTS FROM THE PUBLISHERS

Need and Demand. The majority of the publishers believed that there was a definite need for easy-to-read materials among the adult population in their communities, but that the demand was relatively low.

Effect of Format and Content. The majority believed that the content and use of illustrations were most important factors in making a book appealing to an adult. The next factors mentioned were the size of print and the colour of the illustrations. The size of the illustrations was least frequently mentioned. A few publishers believed that no single factor could affect the readers' choice, but that there is a combination of several factors which makes a book appealing or unappealing to adults.

Recommendations. The respondents suggested that the following requirements must be considered by those involved in the production of easy-to-read materials for adults:

- familiarity with the readers, with their needs, interests and reading abilities;
- well-trained teachers who know the milieu;
- simple language, style, and presentation;
- a basic survey at the start of materials preparation, and evaluation at regular intervals;
- relevance of the content to the needs and interests of the readers;
- publication geared to an educational programme, such as a literacy project or to a government development project;
- coordination of the different stages of production;
- development of a marketing plan or a distribution channel beforehand; and
- active participation of the readers in the development of materials.

CONCLUSIONS

On the basis of the survey, the following conclusions and recommendations can be made.

1. There could be several reasons for the failure of adult literacy programmes in meeting the objectives that were set for them: lack of motivation among the new literates to continue, organizational and pedagogical problems, and lack of appropriate easy-to-read materials (perhaps the most important one). Policy makers should be more concerned about this important task and realize that to spend money on literacy programmes without provision of adequate follow-up materials is a waste of time and effort.

2. Except for a small number, publishers had a relatively low budget. Larger amounts of money must be allocated for this purpose.

3. Publication of easy-to-read materials is not a lucrative enterprise. There is a low market for such materials. This is so because the readers are not able to pay and have not developed their reading habits. It is only after the reading skills of new literates have been reinforced that reading habits can be improved. It is the recognition of this fact that can enable the publishers to produce books for mass consumption. The national and international organizations should increase their subsidies for the publishers of such materials. Literacy instruction, if not substantiated by further follow-up activities, results in relapse and, therefore, leads to a waste of efforts.

4. The producers of easy-to-read materials have to be encouraged and assisted in carrying out more preliminary studies in different areas (reading interest and preference, reading ability, and sociolinguistics) before preparing materials for adults with limited reading ability. Provisions should be made to publish the results of such studies and make them available to all publishers engaged in this task.

5. Publishers usually aim at a nationwide readership and at men. The publishers should be given assistance and subsidies to enable them to aim at local levels, in order to produce

materials which suit the interests of special groups. Distribution of materials should be extended to women. In the Survey of Readers' Interest and Preference carried out by the IIALM, sex was found to be the most definitive variable affecting the adult semiliterates' preferences for different kinds of subject content. Therefore, books on subjects of interest to women should be prepared and distributed.

6. Among the respondents, publishers sponsored by governments did not publish reading materials for linguistic minorities. It is universally recognized that learning in one's mother tongue is easier than in another language. This fact should be emphasized, and the necessary materials should be produced in the indigenous languages.

PART THREE

Issues in Cross-Cultural Cooperation

Cross-cultural cooperation involves the exchange of information and sophisticated research techniques. In discussing international cooperation in educational research, Nisbet (*1*) stated, "The major problem in international cooperation is that research workers from different countries have different attitudes and make different assumptions." Without an opening on a deeper level, little that is truly valuable will be accomplished. The two papers in Part Three address themselves to deeper levels of attitudes, complacencies, emotions, and prejudices.

Chinna Oommen may well be the world's best qualified person to discuss the problems involved in serving as an educational expert in a society not one's own. She has been deeply involved in both receiving and rendering such service. Dr. Oommen was one of the Indian educators who cooperated in, and later directed, the Reading Project initiated by Constance McCullough and who was charged with the development of Hindi textbooks. The Project was designed to serve as a model for the development of texts in the other languages used in India. Subsequently, Oommen served as foreign expert to the Nepalese Government on a similar mission.

Lloyd Kline, in discussing the confusions of translation, points out that there are those things that translate quite well, those that translate only imperfectly, and those that do not translate at all. Kline urges that we "communicate, however, fully realizing all that is lost in translation, neither expecting more than language can deliver, nor communicating other than humbly and gratefully within our imperfection and fallibility."

Reference

1. Nisbet, J. "Comments on the Preliminary Conclusions and Recommendations of the Working Party on Training and Career Structure of Educational Researchers," quoted in a synopsis by the Council of Europe Secretariat, Doc. DECS/RECH (74) 17,11 (1974).

Do's and Don'ts in Serving as a Foreign Expert

Chinna Chacko Oommen
Madras
Tamilnadu, South India

Developing countries depend greatly on the help and services of experts in their programmes of rapid economic and social development and reconstruction of their countries. And so the host or the receiving country looks forward eagerly to the arrival of experts since it requires their expertise, technical knowhow, and methodology in various fields. The success of such programmes depends on many factors, but the major factor is the expert himself, and the way he faces the challenge.

This paper discusses the duties of both the sponsoring and the receiving countries and then presents the Do's and the Don'ts for service as a foreign expert.

DUTIES OF THE SPONSORING
AND HOST COUNTRIES

Prevention is better than cure, so it is the primary function of the sponsoring country to select the best possible person for the job. Certain well thought out criteria should be borne in mind in the selection of the candidate. Care should be taken to check the candidate's professional competence, personal and family background, and reasons for accepting the assignment. Is the candidate professionally competent? Can he impart skills, and has he earned the respect of the people in the field at home?

Does he have the expertise to offer? Can he get along with people, especially people whose culture, habits and language are vastly different from his own? Is he willing to learn? Is his family life happy? Is his desire to help the country his main reason for accepting the job?

All of these aspects are very important for they not only affect the quality of work but, eventually, the relationship between the two countries.

The writer of this paper feels that only the most competent leaders in the field should be sent out to help the poor developing nations for only they can meet the challenge of preparing something effective, useful, and longlasting from the meagre resources and facilities the country can afford.

It is easier for a person to carry on the work in a situation where there is an established order that needs only minor changes or revisions. But when nothing is available, you need a person who can innovate without compromising the ultimate goals.

Only those who have mastery of the subject can delve deeper and plan what needs to be done for the present and for the future. Such a situation demands a person with superb skills, the patience of Job, exceptional insight and expertise. Only he can plant the seed deep enough and nurture it well enough that it can withstand the vicissitudes of nature and the restraining effect of thorns and bushes.

The failure of many programmes around the world due to lack of vision and adequate guidance justifies the concern and plea of the writer for having experts of the highest calibre to help the developing nations.

On the other hand, one can see what a well qualified expert can do in spite of the poor facilities and inadequate resources. For example, in India many attempts have been made in the past to *improve* the reading programme but have been forgotten after the exit of the expert. And it made all the difference in the world when we received an acclaimed leader in the field, one who had the expertise, technical knowhow, vision and patience, and a way of working with people to get the best out of them. The impact is felt not only at the central but the different state levels as well. And one can see the improvement in the reading textbooks and related materials all over the country within the short period of two years. The project has continued and has successfully completed the tasks set aside, even after the expert, Dr. Constance McCullough, left. She achieved this miracle with the help of a team consisting of only five or six members. So it is not just the money nor the facilities available, but the ingenuity and the expertise of the expert that really counts.

It may be difficult to procure the services of top people for an extended period, but an expert can be prevailed upon to accept the job by appealing to his sense of justice, generosity and conviction. One expert was persuaded to leave her work for two years for the opportunity to help the largest democracy in the world, India, representing five hundred million people.

The sponsoring country should send only the best person who can do the job successfully. And the receiving country should settle only for the best. Here is one place I feel "beggers can be chosers." It would help the sponsoring country immensely in their search for the right person if the receiving country would provide a job description of the specific areas of help needed in the country. This information should be prepared and sent to the sponsoring country.

Once the sponsoring country sends the right person, it is the duty of the host country to take full advantage of the great gift they have received. The host country should help the expert get in touch with the leaders in the field; help orient him to the country, its ways, culture, and society. This service should be extended to the expert's family also—getting them settled comfortably and acquainting them with the local markets, initiating them to the variety of social and cultural activities and social work programmes—so that the family can be busy and happy. They should remember that both the expert and his family are part of the success or failure of an assignment, for no expert can give his full attention to any problem when his wife and children are unhappy and are counting the days before returning home.

Assigning a counterpart to work with the expert as soon as he arrives is essential. The expert must have someone to provide ready reference for his queries and for gathering information, collecting data, and working out plans and programmes.

DO'S IN SERVING AS A FOREIGN EXPERT

The expert first should study the problem in all its elements and learn everything he can about the job; the present status, the past history, the good points, and factors that need to be changed. He should learn the educational goals; the developmental and projected plans of the country; achievements so far; and the opinions of the political, social and economic leaders and of people from different walks of life. He should visit classrooms and observe lessons.

If the educational system is different from what the expert is used to, it is well worth his time to check on what is happening currently in the country. The Indian system is based on the British system, so the expert will have an added advantage if he knows what presently is happening in England, especially when he talks to the leading educators of the host country who tend to defend the system most vehemently, oblivious to the fact that the British themselves have made many changes.

The expert should meet with administrators, professors, teachers, and others directly connected with education to share their thinking, ideas, and opinions about solving problems as they see them.

Then the expert must develop a range of options in terms of phasing and cost. A master plan can be prepared, with the help of the team, that will include research to be done; the materials to be prepared such as textbooks, manuals, workbooks, reading materials, tests, and other evaluative materials; the training programme for the staff, teachers, principals, and administrators; and, finally, the revision and reevaluation of the plan. He should develop both long range and short term plans, with time limits outlined. When the expert has to leave, the programme can continue if the plan has been completed.

A word of caution. Generally, experts coming from highly developed countries are not cost conscious. But cost is of vital importance in developing countries and must be considered carefully. When ordering equipment, first make sure whether indigenous materials are available. See whether things can be improvised before ordering.

The expert should love and respect the host country and honour its culture and traditions. He should be a continuous student of the culture in which he is working. Try to get used to the national ways and participate in their functions and festivals, making indigenous materials in furnishing apartments and office, travelling on the national airways and other transportation. He should learn the local language and use it as much as possible. He should not be afraid of mistakes, the language effort as such is appreciated.

Before planning the programme study carefully the indigenous resources and technology. Keep an open mind on methodology. Be willing to learn and work hard on the assignment. A good expert learns as much as he contributes and should be the model in professional etiquette.

The expert should see the good in the system and weave this into the new pattern. He should resist the temptation to change everything but should continue everything that is scientifically sound in the old system. He should accept the idea that in the country to which he is accredited there are equals, if not superiors. There may be a few that are quite good and he should listen to their ideas and opinions on the subject.

One of the primary functions of the expert is to train people to take over his job as fast and as well as possible. "Give not a man a fish, but teach him how to fish." This includes the developing of skills and competencies in others, building up a library, gathering information, collecting data, conducting research, preparing materials, developing strategies, and contacting other parts of the world which do similar work. Again, Dr. McCullough put India on the map of the reading world. Just imagine what we would have missed if she had not put us in touch with the International Reading Association.

It is extremely helpful if the expert records specific directions and suggestions for the successful completion of the different assignments envisaged and undertaken by the project. In countries where no such directions were given, the work suffered and the project dwindled away after the expert left; the finished product was vastly different from what it was meant to be. No expert can stay until the project is completed, nor tell everything one needs to know about the job during the short period of training. Hence the need for recording specific directions.

Preparation of Textbooks in the Mother Tongue by Constance McCullough is such a document. And without any hesitation, I can say this volume is one of the reasons the reading project in India was completed successfully after the expert left. Our expert not only trained the staff but wrote the specific directions which enabled the staff to go on with the project. As there is always a great dearth of experts in the country, this written document served us as an expert in absentia and, incidentally, helped not only other projects in our country but also a great many reading projects around the world. International Reading Association published the volume and copies are available at the International Reading Association's Headquarters in Newark, Delaware.

It is also a good idea to keep in touch with the "adopted child." Again, in India we were lucky and our expert was in close touch with our project and constantly kept us informed of the latest trends in the field and about areas that needed change and revision.

DON'TS IN SERVING AS A FOREIGN EXPERT

Try to remember that the duty of the expert is not to work for but to work with the country. Try not to be condescending. Develop a co-worker relationship. Remember it should not always be "my good way and another's bad way."

Don't accept an assignment in a foreign country if you do not genuinely care for that country and sincerely desire to help the country.

Don't accept a position if you do not feel technically competent. Don't bluff or pretend, others will find you out sooner or later.

Do not make a gift of a lot of unessential equipment. Developing countries have a weakness for asking for a lot of equipment and often the expert is tolerated only as a necessary evil accompanying the equipment. Don't be in a hurry to order unless there is a compelling need for equipment and the local people can illustrate the way in which the equipment is to be used.

Don't take an assignment thinking that the assignment is likely to remove a personal problem. Stay at home and control your frustration before venturing on a difficult journey. One can do a better job then.

Try not to make the mistake of thinking that since the receiving country's development is very low in the area, work will be somewhat light and that one can look forward to having a paid holiday. Nothing is more wrong than this.

Don't believe in the banking theory of knowledge. Don't feel that the expert has the wisdom which the virgin soil lacks. Don't underestimate the audience's abilities.

Resist the temptation of coming to the host country with the expert's own projects, thinking that the virgin soil is the ground for data collection. This not only diverts attention from the work but reinforces the feeling that the people of this country are informants.

Don't let political biases come in the way of cultural sharing. It is good to know and to be aware of the power bases. But it is unfortunate if the expert is exclusively identified with such power.

It is human weakness to favour openly someone who has been of great help to the expert in his work. This is good, but unfortunately it creates jealousy among the coworkers and the life of the favoured coworker could become miserable after the expert leaves.

Due to lack of space I have offered here only a few important points for experts.

I conclude by thanking the following people who very graciously took time to discuss this topic with me. They include people who were experts themselves in more than one country, officers who were in charge of hiring experts both in the host and the sponsoring countries, and people who have worked with experts: Reginald Bell, D.P. Pattanayak, R. Viswasm, M.F. Stough, Alagappan, R.N. Mehrotra, C.M. McCullough, A. Chari, and C.T.A. Pillai.

That Which is Lost in Translation

Lloyd W. Kline
International Reading Association
Newark, Delaware
United States of America

In exploring my topic, "That Which Is Lost in Translation," I have discovered that much of what there is to say about it must come from the individual heart—yours as well as mine—rather than from the experimental laboratory. I suppose I should apologize for that fact, since we are a group of educators and scholars hoping to exchange demonstrated truths in the spirit of scientific inquiry. But I will not apologize, for to do so would be to deny whatever cluster of possible truths I think I have identified in my exploration.

Briefly, I discovered very early that to ask questions about translation is to inquire into the nature of language—its origins, its characteristics, its uses. One is led quickly away from rather simple scientific fact into legend and belief, philosophy and poetry. I am convinced that the ultimate truths one discovers about translation are the ancient truths of paradox and mystery. They are uttered more appropriately, perhaps, by oracles than by scientists. Only circumstantially do they deal with differences among languages. Essentially, they deal with one of the basic questions of human existence: Do we live our lives as complete individuals, perceiving our own unique worlds and thinking our own distinctive thoughts in patterns that can be shared only partially and imperfectly with anyone else? Or do we live our lives as both products and members of a social and physical environment, a measurable universe defined in certain terms by the collective experience of the human beings who inhabit it?

All this sounds presumptuous on my part, but let me hasten to assure you that I did begin a systematic review of the literature at the onset of my study and that I intended a thoroughly detailed, purely rational, painfully objective, very impersonal argument. But I gave up both pursuits when they proved less than sufficient to the task at hand.

Instead, I will tell you the source of my title, "That Which Is Lost in Translation." It was at a summer session for graduate students in English in the late 1950s that I first heard American poet Robert Frost define poetry as "that which is lost in translation." I will tell you the more immediate stimulus for my offering to explore the topic of translation here. First as International Reading Association journals editor, later as director of publications, I have sat somewhere near the center of all those proposals that would have us disseminate the words we speak as an Association in numerous other languages as well as in English. And I will share with you some observations about how and why language should be taught.

The characteristic problems of translation are not a new topic to me nor to humanity. I was first introduced to the general idea of language differences as a very young child, through repetition in Christian church school of that ancient passage from the Old Testament of the Holy Bible, the story of the Tower of Babel. Whatever your religion, you probably know the tale. The "whole earth was of one language and of one speech." The people decided to build a city and a tower that would reach heaven. The chief architect in heaven itself, however, apparently had grave misgivings, for the Lord noted that with such ambitious plans in their hearts, the people would be restrained from nothing they could imagine to do. Therefore, the Lord confounded the people's language so that they might not understand one another's speech, and "the Lord scattered them abroad from thence upon the face of all the earth."

Needless to say, we have never recovered.

Those of us who specialize in reading and writing are so caught up in the study of what language is and does that we forget what it is not and what it cannot do. Like those Old Testament descendents of Noah, we sometimes let our aspirations overwhelm our capabilities. Our expectations of language as means of communication probably exceed its capacity to communicate. We might be so proficient at verbalizing that we verbalize beyond reality. Perhaps we need a prophet to point out the confusion of tongues among us and remind us of that which is lost in translation—so much the sadder for all of us, we so easily assume.

Sad? Is it really sad to recognize that language has its limitations as well as its benefits? Look into your own experience.

I was born and raised in a region marked by anything but linguistic purity. First of all, my native language is that hybrid of hybrids, that chameleon of chameleons, English! Anyone who has studied the English language knows you cannot count very long on anything like consistency and stability within the English language. Put two or three words together in English and you probably have come up with a Germanic structure, a Romance vocabulary, and spelling and pronunciation conventions from just about anywhere in the world.

But there is more to my background. Quirk of fortune that it was for me to have been born into a primarily English language heritage, many of the friends, family, and neighbors of my childhood spoke various degrees of that parochial twentieth century phenomenon known as Pennsylvania Dutch. More properly, Pennsylvania Dutch is a diverse collection of mutations of Palatinate German. It survives within a relatively few square miles of the eastern United States from the seventeeth century German of a group of religious dissenters who fled their European origins in the name of freedom, to the glory of God, and in the heat of individual conscience.

To this day, pronunciations and spellings for a given object may differ from farm to farm in that area. Indeed, in my childhood, while I cannot blame the confusion solely on the Pennsylvania Dutch, you could not be sure if you should call such a common object as a paper bag a bag, a sack, a toot, or a poke. One or the other "misnomer" might even earn you a dirty look, if not a cuff on the ear. Little did I know as a child that when I talked about spritzing the grass, few outside my immediate geographic region would know that I was talking about watering the lawn. And I was very much into middle age before I learned quite abruptly that one of the innocent and quite onomatopoetic Dutch colloquialisms of my childhood denotes a very obscene function for certain citizens of San Francisco, a continent removed from my childhood.

So, my own experience tells me that we will survive the confusion of languages that looms as an impossible barrier among us. Translation is, after all, one of humankind's miracles. While we have not yet accomplished the dream of Babel, to enter and exit the gates of heaven at will, we have been able to enter each other's hearts and minds almost at will. Tolstoy is available in many different languages now and, thanks to paperbacks and print technology, he is available rather inexpensively to most of us in industrialized nations. We are able to share approximate re-creations of other times and other worlds and other minds through the commonplace miracle of print translation. How much truer today can Shakespeare's statement be that nothing human is foreign to me. Almost all we need to do is choose the right book in the right translation, open it, and read.

Perhaps it is this easy access to translation which prompts me to call attention for a moment away from the comforting miracle, to remind us that translation is not so easy a process as is our access to it, to point out that much is lost in translation, to ponder, as John Guthrie has called my theme in this address, "the withered edges of the flower." In more prosaic terms, there are those things which translate quite well and easily, both between individuals and across languages. There are those things that translate only imperfectly. And there are those things that do not translate at all. Let me offer some examples of each.

The latter day pictographs that one sees with increasing frequency as directional signs in air terminals, in subways, and on highways are dramatic evidence that we human beings can, indeed, communicate across languages a considerable body of common experience with a high degree of accuracy and usefulness—some might say by circumventing language in the traditional sense of letters, words, and sentences. Men's and ladies' rest rooms, of course, were among the first facilities to be identified not by word, but by graphic symbol. A host of similar graphic symbols have followed in public places very quickly and very effectively. I have read that at the 1976 Olympic Games in Montreal, 26 sports activities and 173 other informational or service messages were conveyed by pictograph alone. They included such diverse messages as money exchange, meeting points, bathtubs, locker rooms, customs inspection, interviewing, pet and litter prohibition, lost children, and where to get sponges. I am sure that some of the signs were misinterpreted by some of the people who looked at them, but consider the number of words and hopeless conversations they saved, the number of people who were helped.

Lover of language that I am, I must confess that in driving my automobile, I much prefer graphic symbols to words—except for place names, of course. Tell me that I should not turn left simply by showing me a black or white arrow with a red X across it, or to proceed with caution by showing me a blinking yellow light. Please do not force me at highway speed to decode, interpret, and obey an ambiguous sign that says in block letters only, "SLOW TRAFFIC RIGHT TURN LEFT CENTER LANE ONLY."

Certainly, some experiences translate well and the ease of such visual communication—closely akin to the universal kinesics of the smile, the open hand, the simulated cup at the lips—leads us to yearn for an international alphabet and a universal language. However, what we too often forget is that what is most universal in our collective experience and, thus, most easily communicated by gestures and signs as well as by utterances, is also most concrete, by and large. Or it is most abstract and specialized, as are the mathematical symbols recognized worldwide by the relatively few mathematicians among us. Unfortunately, between the basic physical facts that lead us to rest rooms, food stands, lost children, and sponges, and the rather esoteric information conveyed by the symbols of theoretical mathematics, lies that vast realm where most of us live and move and have our being, where most of us really care about communicating.

The movement in language evolution from concrete to abstract, but not so far toward abstract as to be generally useless, takes us very quickly into approximation rather than exactitude. That inevitability was brought home to me quite vividly the first time I compared translations of the Lord's Prayer in Old English, Middle English, Elizabethan English and twentieth century American, respectively. "Forgive us our *guilt*" turned into *trespass* and then into *debt* and, finally, into the ultimate concept of today's credit card society, "Forgive us what we owe you." The tangible *loaf* generalized into *daily bread*, then abstracted into *our daily needs*. Where is the eternal truth in such transition of word and concept from tongue to tongue, place to place, century to century within little more than a thousand years? To cite a second example, would the original concept of the Latinate word *expedite* be translated into English more faithfully by the contemporary slang phrase *kick it off* (off or from the foot) than by the more sophisticated and equally Latinate *to execute promptly?*

Yet, language does seem to serve to pass information from generation to generation, culture to culture. As various semanticists have pointed out, unlike chimpanzees each one of us does not need to touch fire to realize that it burns us if we touch it too long. We can be forewarned through language by "Don't touch!" Yet, who among us has not been burned, nonetheless? Who has not tested the linguistic hypothesis? Maybe we satisfy a basic need to experience first before accepting the language. Much of our scientific attitude and practice, after all, has been developed to check hypotheses that verbal tradition tells us to accept without question: "Kill all snakes." "Tomatoes are poisonous." "The world was made in six days."

So, we have moved inexorably into my second category: What is it that translates only with great imperfection, risk, and difficulty?

The many different Eskimo words for *snow* are cited quite often to illustrate how one's experience affects one's vocabulary. It also demonstrates one of the central problems of translation. While I find the English word *influence* quite positive in its connotations, Egal Ali, my Somalian colleague, has educated me to the fact that it holds most unfortunate connotations for many in the world whose nations are not among the few so-called superpowers, who sometimes use influence most heavyhandedly. Hap Gilliland told me of an Amazon tribe he met for whom death itself is a taboo. Thus, there is no record possible among them of either population growth or depletion, no sense of ancestor or heir.

Faced with cultural differences of such magnitude and depth, is it any wonder that translation leads to imperfect communication at best? The greater mystery is why we do not completely miscommunicate more often in shifting from language to language. In discussing the mass infusion of Latin word roots into English during the European Renaissance, Baugh (2:259) writes, "The very act of translation brings home to the translator the limitations of his medium and tempts him to borrow from other languages the terms whose lack he feels in his own."

Sapir (*13*) reminds us that language itself, whether or not it undergoes translation, is singularly *not* adept at expressing the emotions of life. It is very good in communicating the rational, structured, ordered, predictable sides of life. It carries thought well, emotion poorly. Because humor depends on both cultural context and emotional response, much of it tends to translate very poorly. I suppose every language has its idiomatic rituals that cannot possibly be translated. The iconoclast in me fights many of those rituals even among fellow speakers of my own native tongue. "How are you?" an American asks, never expecting any answer other than "Fine, thank you," even if you are on your deathbed. A friend of mine, knowing that most Americans automatically couple salt with pepper at the table, used to bark his request: "Pass the salt, please—*not* the pepper; just the salt!"

I am convinced that Esperanto, Volapük, and other attempts at artificial international languages have failed to gain wide acceptance and use for similar reasons. They have been purely rational attempts when much of what we treasure in our own native tongues is idiomatic, even irrational. They must be imposed artificially when much of our native expression is contextual, spontaneous, and idiosyncratic.

Such thoughts lead me to consider a few of those things that do not translate at all.

The truth of Frost's definition of poetry as "that which is lost in translation" was best demonstrated to me in the reading in class of two separate English translations of the same French poem, "Letter from Mexico," by Tristan Corbiére. In my severely limited ability to read French, I caught only the essential facts of the poem: A young soldier had died of a fever and his sergeant was writing to inform his family. From the two English translations, both rendered by English speaking poets who knew French better than I, I caught all sorts of things unavailable to me in my reading of the French itself: moods, nuances, tones, certain rhythms, pauses, other sound techniques, attitudes, orientation, characterizations—all these I had missed, essentially, in my restricted ability to read the French original.

The episode would probably not have remained with me to this day, however, if I had not learned a more startling lesson during the experience. The two English translations were as obviously different from each other as either of them was from the original French! There is more lost in translation—any translation of just about anything worth translating—than is communicated. The best rendering of a message from language to language is not an act of translation so much as it is an admirable attempt at approximate re-creation of another's experience.

That struck me as a rather sad lesson, a stark disillusionment, until I was able to understand that it only reflects from language to language what is also true from person to person, print to mind. As I heard Leland Jacobs say so eloquently, "Reading is bringing meaning to and taking meaning from a page of print." Meaning in language never is solely a one-way phenomenon, just as perfect translation is at last impossible. Even voice patterns have been found to be individually distinctive to the individuals whose lips and tongues and throats have created them—at least as unique to individuals as are fingerprints. Your reading of something someone else has written is as peculiar to you as the writing was to the writer. What you read is certainly quite different from what that person wrote, since neither of you can bring exactly the same meaning to the page in exactly the same voice and mindset.

Does all this mean that we should give up on all translation? Of course not, no more than we should quit talking to each other within our own language groups. We should communicate, however, fully realizing all that is lost in translation, neither expecting more than language can deliver nor communicating other than humbly and gratefully within our imperfection and fallibility. The drive for translation, for universal communication, is as much a quest after the imperfectible as the various projects of Don Quixote are unattainable. Yet, it is such a quest that makes us and keeps us human.

Teachers, I suspect, rarely get into these human facts of language with their students. The problems of translation, the limitations of language, disturbing little questions of approximation, cultural differences, linguistic relativity, are swamped by one-choice answer keys, absolute misstatements of rule, and narrow exercises. If we really understood and cared about language, we would see it and teach it in its imperfection as well as in its various predictable patterns. The experience would remind us that specialists, for all the highly focused expertise they can bring to narrowly defined problems, do not, after all, live in a vacuum. We need to hear what they say to us from their artificially confined laboratories, but we will put their findings into more useful perspective if we live broadly and listen carefully.

We need to request translation with our economic eyes wide open for, in this age of cost accounting, money is as much a factor as any idealistic dream of international cooperation. To reproduce a document in a second or a third language—indeed, to produce it in a first language—is to ask how much it will cost to deliver to how many people with what promise of financial recovery. Returning for a moment to schools, how often have we introduced the teaching of second and third languages as a literary or cultural activity, when the decisions about which second or third languages to teach have been motivated fundamentally by economics and politics rather than by culture, with its esthetic connotations of art and literature?

Facing great odds and reservations and limitations, why do we who are neither politicians nor merchants persist so strongly in our drive for translation? Is it a fear of loneliness? Do we yearn to speak to and be spoken to by others? Anything but the thought of being alone in an unresponsive universe! Our engineers bounce radio signals from Mars and Jupiter and send them to galaxies unseen, while the odds are astronomical against any living organism waiting out there, capable of understanding the message.

Or perhaps we are impelled by a vague, unspoken suspicion that because we do not speak another's language, someone knows something we don't know, something that might assuage the loneliness or remind us that someone cares, that we are not alone, or, finally, assure us that the other person knows no more than we know.

Perhaps our egos intrude. My language is my own. To speak to me in your own tongue, which is not my own, and expect me to follow what you say is to put my language down, exalt your own, and denigrate me a bit in the process.

Or perhaps we just reject, at last, the notion that not only translation but language itself is bedevilled by limitations, that all communication serves sooner or later to remind us of what we cannot communicate. Perhaps we believe that if only we become more prolific and adept with translation, all of us will share some common absolute truth that will once and for all overwhelm the ignorance of the world. Perhaps our trouble is that we dream large dreams, think smaller thoughts, and discover too few words to convey either dreams or thoughts sufficiently to someone else.

What we need to satisfy our soulful yearning to hear and be heard, I believe, is not translation of the word so much as sharing of the spirit in our quest for communication. We need to exchange information, yes, but knowing full well that the spirit of exchange is probably more significant than the information itself. We need to acknowledge our anxieties (if they exist), our fears of loneliness, our suspicions that someone knows something we don't know, our feelings of inferiority and alienation when we are treated as linguistic foreigners. But we need to acknowledge them in the faith that all of us share similar anxieties, and that such is the human condition, that all of us are linguistically higher than the apes, certainly, but somewhat lower than the angels in their wordless adoration of eternal truth. We need to acknowledge that common human condition of always being somewhere in-between, recognizing the acknowledgment as more important than the imperfect communication of anything we think we might know or want to know.

A contemporary African poet, G. Adali-Mortty (*1*), has said it well in "Belonging":

> You may excel
> in knowledge of their tongue,
> and universal ties may bind you close to them;
> but what they say, and how they feel—
> the subtler details of their meaning,
> thinking, feeling, reaching—
> these are closed to you and me for evermore;
> as are, indeed, the interleaves of speech
> —our speech— which fall on them
> no more than were they dead leaves
> in dust-dry harmattan,
> although, for years, they've lived
> and counted all there is to count
> in our midst!

References

1. Adali-Mortty, G. "Belonging," in Kofi Awoonor and G. Adali-Mortty (Eds.), *Messages: Poems from Ghana*. London: Heinemann Educational Books.
2. Baugh, Albert C. *A History of the English Language,* Second Edition. New York: Appleton-Century-Crofts, 1957.
3. Chao, Yuen Ren. *Language and Symbolic Systems*. Cambridge: Cambridge University Press, 1968.
4. Cherry, Colin. *On Human Communication: A Review, a Survey, and a Criticism*. Cambridge: MIT Press, 1966.
5. Chomsky, Noam. *Language and Mind*. New York: Harcourt Brace Jovanovich, 1972.
6. Clark, John T. *Lexicological Evoluton and Conceptual Progress*. Berkeley: University of California Press, 1918.
7. Deese, James Earle. *Psycholinguistics*. Boston: Allyn and Bacon, 1970.
8. Gibson, Walker (Ed.). *The Limits of Language*. New York: Hill and Wang, 1962.
9. Griffin, Willis H., and Ralph B. Spence. *Cooperative International Education*. Washington, D.C.: Association for Supervision and Curriculum Development, 1970.
10. Landar, Herbert Jay. *Language and Culture*. New York: Oxford University Press, 1965.
11. Quine, Willard Van Orman. *Word and Object*. Cambridge: MIT Press, 1960.
12. Richards, I. A. *Speculative Instruments*. Chicago: University of Chicago Press, 1955.
13. Sapir, Edward. *Language*. New York: Harcourt Brace Jovanovich, 1921.
14. Wittgenstein, Ludwig. *The Blue and Brown Books*. New York: Harper and Row, 1958.